DEVELOPMENT CENTRE STUDIES

CONFLICT AND GROWTH IN AFRICA

Vol. 2: Kenya, Tanzania and Uganda

By
Jeni Klugman, Bilin Neyapti
and
Frances Stewart

DEVELOPMENT CENTRE
OF THE ORGANISATION FOR ECONOMIC CO-OPERATION AND DEVELOPMENT

ORGANISATION FOR ECONOMIC CO-OPERATION AND DEVELOPMENT

Pursuant to Article 1 of the Convention signed in Paris on 14th December 1960, and which came into force on 30th September 1961, the Organisation for Economic Co-operation and Development (OECD) shall promote policies designed:

- to achieve the highest sustainable economic growth and employment and a rising standard of living in Member countries, while maintaining financial stability, and thus to contribute to the development of the world economy;
- to contribute to sound economic expansion in Member as well as non-member countries in the process of economic development; and
- to contribute to the expansion of world trade on a multilateral, non-discriminatory basis in accordance with international obligations.

The original Member countries of the OECD are Austria, Belgium, Canada, Denmark, France, Germany, Greece, Iceland, Ireland, Italy, Luxembourg, the Netherlands, Norway, Portugal, Spain, Sweden, Switzerland, Turkey, the United Kingdom and the United States. The following countries became Members subsequently through accession at the dates indicated hereafter: Japan (28th April 1964), Finland (28th January 1969), Australia (7th June 1971), New Zealand (29th May 1973), Mexico (18th May 1994), the Czech Republic (21st December 1995), Hungary (7th May 1996), Poland (22nd November 1996) and Korea (12th December 1996). The Commission of the European Communities takes part in the work of the OECD (Article 13 of the OECD Convention).

The Development Centre of the Organisation for Economic Co-operation and Development was established by decision of the OECD Council on 23rd October 1962 and comprises twenty-three Member countries of the OECD: Austria, Belgium, Canada, the Czech Republic, Denmark, Finland, France, Germany, Greece, Iceland, Ireland, Italy, Japan, Korea, Luxembourg, Mexico, the Netherlands, Norway, Poland, Portugal, Spain, Sweden and Switzerland, as well as Argentina and Brazil from March 1994, and Chile since November 1998. The Commission of the European Communities also takes part in the Centre's Advisory Board.

The purpose of the Centre is to bring together the knowledge and experience available in Member countries of both economic development and the formulation and execution of general economic policies; to adapt such knowledge and experience to the actual needs of countries or regions in the process of development and to put the results at the disposal of the countries by appropriate means.

The Centre has a special and autonomous position within the OECD which enables it to enjoy scientific independence in the execution of its task. Nevertheless, the Centre can draw upon the experience and knowledge available in the OECD in the development field.

338.96
C748
VOL. 2

Publié en français sous le titre :

CONFLITS ET CROISSANCE EN AFRIQUE
Vol. 2 : Kenya, Ouganda et Tanzanie

*
* *

Foreword

This publication is produced in the context of the Development Centre's work on seeking ways to integrate poorer countries into the world economy. It results specifically from the project entitled *Political Economy and Development in Africa*. Two other volumes complete the series.

Acknowledgements

The Development Centre would like to express its gratitude to the Government of Switzerland for the financial support given to the project on "Emerging Africa" in the context of which this study was carried out.

Table of Contents

East Africa – Tanzania, Kenya and Uganda

The boundaries and names shown on this map do not imply official endorsement or acceptance by the OECD.

Preface

The importance of the socio-political environment for African countries was highlighted in the conclusions of a 1994 Development Centre seminar entitled "What Future for Africa?". Indeed, for many African countries, economic failures are the result of political instability, violence and civil wars which have paralysed their societies.

The Centre's research programme on the causes and consequences of conflict in Africa was undertaken in this context. Three regions were selected for analysis, and this study focuses on Kenya, Tanzania and Uganda; two further studies examine countries of West and of Southern Africa. The resulting comparison is interesting as these three countries, which had similar levels of development in 1960, had quite different experiences over the following three decades: peace in Tanzania; relative peace in Kenya punctuated by sporadic violence; and horrific civil war in Uganda with hundreds of thousands of deaths. By comparing these countries' histories, the authors are able to identify the causes and estimate the costs of conflict.

Uganda's economy was ruined by war. Viewed as the most promising of the three countries during the colonial period, Uganda has seen the living standards of its people plummet so far that it is now the poorest. Occasional violence in Kenya, however, failed to compromise growth which remained strong until recent years when it began to take a toll, alongside other factors, on the country's development. Tanzania experienced poor economic performance in the 1970s and 1980s, but this was due to economic policy errors. Indeed, policies pursued in the 1960s and 1990s produced better performance. This three-country comparison demonstrates that political instability has a very high cost, once it goes beyond a certain level.

The originality of this study lies in the unique political-economic analysis used by the authors to bring out factors which influence political stability and instability. Colonial policy in Uganda was responsible for the deep political and economic cleavage between the Bantu south and the multi-ethnic north, creating a potentially explosive political situation following independence. Social spending for health and education had been concentrated in the south, allowing this region to develop a commercial class, whereas the north had been looked upon only as an area to supply workers and soldiers. At the opposite end of the spectrum, Tanzania did not suffer from such a dichotomy at independence. In addition, subsequent governments actively promoted national integration and strove for a balanced public-spending policy which would benefit all regions and all ethnic groups.

This comparison illustrates that for these countries economic inequality at the outset played a role in generating conflict, but once conflict had begun, the situation became much more complex. Religious, ethnic or political friction was exploited to aggravate tension and once massacres began, society was plunged into a cycle of hatred and revenge.

The best strategy is therefore one of prevention and the authors seek to identify several avenues to achieve this end. The overriding goal of this study is to help avoid the massacres and misery which ravage war-torn countries. It will no doubt stimulate the interest of a wide readership.

Ulrich Hiemenz
Director
OECD Development Centre
July 1999

Executive Summary

How far do economic and social disparities explain whether nations become politically stable or unstable, peaceful or violent, compared with other factors, such as differences in colonial heritage, political systems and the vagaries of individual leaders? This book explores that question in the histories of three African countries — Kenya, Tanzania and Uganda — which offer vivid contrasts in both the outcomes and their possible causes over more than three decades of post-independence history. The three, all ex-British colonies, began independence with roughly similar economic development strategies but then diverged markedly in policy implementation, economic growth and the achievement of economic and social equity within their systems. They also have had radically different experiences with political stability and violent conflict. Making sense of these varied outcomes within consistent causal hypotheses may help to illuminate the situations of other countries, in Africa and elsewhere.

The book argues that the economic motivation for conflict depends on how both leaders and followers — in groups because groups, not individuals, carry out organised violence — perceive its economic costs and benefits. Both involve control over resources, to which horizontal inequality (inequities between or among groups) has more importance than absolute access because conflict happens when one group attacks another to improve its relative position. Non-economic factors come into play when ethnic or cultural divisions and political events are seized upon as instruments to cultivate and use in order to seek power.

The evidence largely bears out the argument, in national contexts replete with ever-changing complexities. The strongest form of its conclusions lies in its contention that economic-inspired violence requires both leaders and followers to perceive that they have so little to lose that the potential gains outweigh the losses. This often obtained in Uganda because economic opportunities outside the state were so slight that control over the state became all-important; peasants received so few social or economic benefits from the market system that they could retreat into subsistence activity with relatively little loss. In Kenya, however, potential leaders could prosper economically without political power, hence without violence, while enough peasants gained enough from the system in income growth and basic services to give them an interest in stability; social stratification was vertical, with the very poor and the middle class found in a number of ethnic groups. Tanzania from the start incorporated members

9

of different ethnic groups into its large civil service and made its expanding basic social services (health and education, largely) universally available; these gains lessened and even reversed in the late 1970s and early 1980s, but groups shared the emergent losses evenly.

These forces illuminate the outcomes. Tanzania has had remarkable political stability and absence of conflict; Kenya has felt tensions but remained relatively free of violent conflict; and Uganda holds one of the continent's worst records of recurrent mass violence — tempered in recent years by a regime which has changed the economic calculus of costs and benefits towards stability and less violent political strife.

Chapter 1

Introduction:
The Analytical Framework

This book explores whether differences in socio-economic conditions can explain markedly different records of political stability and violence better than other factors such as differences in colonial heritage, political systems and the roles of individual leaders. It tests the hypothesis that the relative economic positions of groups in society greatly influence the extent of instability and conflict. Conflicts in Africa result from a complex interaction among ethnic, regional and religious divisions, but entrenched economic differences within these societies underlie these distinctions. Even where individual leaders and/or ethnic divisions have importance, economic factors may provide the motivation that leads to conflict.

Since their independence in the 1960s, the three East African countries — all ex-British colonies — have had radically different experiences with political instability, violent conflict and patterns of economic and social development. Tanzania has shown remarkable political stability and absence of conflict. Kenya has felt considerable tensions but still remained relatively free of violent conflict compared to neighbouring Uganda, which holds one of the continent's worst records of recurrent mass violence, involving the deaths of some 800 000. The three have also had major differences in development strategies and outcomes. All chose fairly interventionist import-substitution regimes immediately after independence and aimed to extend basic social services universally, but performances differed markedly as both political developments and policy implementation strategies diverged.

Kenya and Uganda, subject to British colonial rule from the late nineteenth century, along with Tanzania, formed through a union of Tanganyika and Zanzibar in 1964, had made up the East Africa Protectorate. The British had acquired control of Tanganyika in 1920 after German colonisation from 1885. Each country gained political independence in the early 1960s. At that time they had similar populations (Uganda's was smallest, at 8 million). Each contained a number of tribal groups, mostly speaking different languages. The relatively larger ethnic groupings in Kenya and Uganda had local administrative boundaries drawn around them. Kenya had higher average per capita incomes in 1960, but not among its Africans; the difference arose from non-African incomes. All three had similar social indicators such as life expectancy, adult literacy and access to safe water. These initial broad similarities make a comparison of the paths of post-independence events particularly illuminating. Kenya and Uganda hold special interest because of their apparently strong similarities in ethnic tensions among sizeable groups. The first part of the book focuses on them, with one large chapter devoted to Tanzania and a concluding one which covers all three and offers lessons for both domestic policy makers and international donors.

The Framework for Analysis

The motivation and execution of violent conflict need to be understood at two levels. Organised, violent conflicts have leaders, who instigate and orchestrate them, and followers who carry them out, acquiesce, or provide shelter for fighters. Sustained conflict requires support at both levels. The economic motivation for conflict depends on how both potential leaders and their prospective followers perceive its economic costs and benefits, especially the prospects for control over resources. For potential leaders, this means control over decisions about jobs, contracts and so on; the achievement of power promises personal economic gains and the ability to reward associated groups. For followers, access to resources includes income earning opportunities (employment), assets (especially land), social services, etc. Conflict becomes most likely when the calculus of costs and benefits perceived by both groups favours it.

Normally, perceptions broadly reflect reality. Consequently, one can evaluate the actual economic situations of groups in dimensions relevant to calculations about gains and losses from conflict. These include access to assets, employment and state benefits that give rise to a range of economic and social entitlements. Factors underlying these entitlements include aggregate trends in economic and human development, the structure of the economy, population/resource ratios, public policies towards expenditure and taxation, and entitlement rules (such as property rights, or rights to democratic participation).

Relative access is likely to have more importance than absolute access, because conflict involves one group's attacking another to improve its relative position. Hence degrees of inequality need assessment. Yet inequality alone is not usually a sufficient cause of conflict; other conditions must also be present. First, both leaders and followers must perceive inequities as sufficiently great that the gains from fighting will exceed its costs. Second, the government may itself instigate violence, or have insufficient strength to repress it quickly. Third, those who fight need access to support, such as weapons and food. Fourth, the degree of economic integration also plays a role. Groups' potential gains and losses from conflict relate not only to their absolute or relative entitlements, but also to how they might lose them as a result of it. In a weakly integrated economy, a collapse brought on by conflict may have only a small economic impact on individuals because they can generate income without much trade or exchange. With more economic integration, the costs of conflict will rise as individuals or groups lose capacity for self-provisioning.

This framework does not deny the relevance of non-economic factors. It hypothesises that normally there is some underlying economic motivation for violent power-seeking, with ethnic or cultural divisions and political events as important instruments cultivated and used for this end. A political system that permits non-violent change will make violence an unnecessarily costly way of bringing about change. Political entitlements thus become relevant, including access to decision-making mechanisms at the local and national levels and such basic human rights as freedom from arbitrary detention, right of assembly and free speech.

By definition, groups carry out organised violence, not individuals acting randomly as is the case with much crime. The groups must perceive themselves as such, with a common interest in violence, although people may be pressured into joining a group and taking to force. The analysis therefore needs to categorise interests by groups, which may differ in ethnicity, religion, geography or economic class, or some combination of these. This work considers each type of differentiation, but the frequent use of ethnicity to explain violence in these countries calls for an initial survey of the main ethnic differences.

Groups and Ethnic Composition in East Africa

Mugai (1995, p. 161) has defined ethnicity as "the consciousness among people who share cultural and linguistic, sometimes kinship and religious, roots (and who conditionally affiliate for purposes of political action)". Other analysts suggest ethnicity involves the joint maximisation of the political, economic and social interests of the group (see, for example, Chazan et al., 1992).

In Kenya and Uganda, ethnicity dominates group formation, while it has much less significance in Tanzania. For example, Mugai (1995, p 168) argues that in Kenya, the "masses openly and consciously express their ethnic solidarity in the workplace, in schools, in hospitals and at political rallies". In each country, other divisions, religious and economic, cut across the ethnic divisions. Kenya has 30 officially recognised ethnic groups ranging in size from a few hundred to several million people. The five largest, each with more than a million members and together comprising more than 70 per cent of the population, include in order of size: Kikuyu, Luyha, Luo, Kalenjin and Kamba. Uganda at independence had 15 major ethnic groups, speaking an estimated 63 languages or dialects. These divided broadly between Bantu (South) and non-Bantu (North) languages under a European classification not previously recognised by Africans, while the Nilotic (West Nile) formed a third category. Prior to colonialism, four of the groups, Buganda, Bunyoro, Kitara and Nkore (inhabited by Ankole), had centralised kingdoms organised on hierarchical lines, a pattern maintained in the colonial period. Other groups formed "segmentary" societies, more egalitarian with no central authority, including Lango, Acholi, Lugbara and Kakwa in the North and East. Tanzania too has great ethnic diversity with roughly 120 tribal groups speaking a variety of languages, although 95 per cent of its native Africans have Bantu origin. The largest,

Sukuma, accounts for less than one-twelfth of the population[1]. The other relatively large tribes each constitute between 3 and 5 per cent of the population and thus no single ethnic group dominates.

The number, magnitude and geographic distribution of ethnic groups do not differ much between Kenya and Uganda (Table 1.1). The largest group in each (the Kikuyu in Kenya and the Buganda in Uganda) are of significant size but cannot form a majority without allies. The same holds for Tanzania, but here the largest group forms a much smaller share of the population (around 8 per cent compared with roughly 20 per cent and 30 per cent in Kenya and Uganda respectively). Hence a democratic system in each country requires a "composed" majority, which potentially alternative groupings could achieve. A non-democratic setting also would be likely to require incorporation of a spread of ethnicities for stability. Ostensibly, this type of ethnic composition might seem less liable to violence than the majority/minority situations of Rwanda, Burundi or Northern Ireland, where the majority can easily oppress the minority with no democratic redress, or than a polity with all groupings so small that deals cannot be brokered. While the Kenyan and Tanzanian stories support this view, Uganda shows that such deals can easily break down and disintegrate into violence and retaliation.

Table 1.1. The Size and Location of the Largest Ethnic Groups in Kenya and Uganda

Kenya			Uganda		
Ethnic Group	Per Cent of Population (1989)	Provincial Location	Ethnic Group	Per Cent of African Population (1969)	Regional Location
Kikuyu	20.8	Central	Buganda	28.2	Southern
Luyha	14.4	Western	Banyanko	12.2	Western
Luo	12.4	Nyanza	Basogo	10.0	Eastern
Kalenjin	11.5	Rift Valley	Batoro	6.1	Western
Kamba	11.4	Eastern-South	Nubians	6.1	Northern-West Nile
Kisii	6.2		Bakedi	5.6	Eastern
Meru	5.1		Langi	5.3	Northern
Masai	1.8	Rift Valley-South	Acholi	4.9	Northern
Embu	1.2	Eastern-Central	Bagisu	4.5	Eastern

Sources: Statistics Department, Ministry of Finance and Economic Planning, Kampala; Republic of Kenya, Population Census 1989; Middleton and Rassam, 1990.

Note

1. According to the national census of 1957 (Hyden, 1986, p. 39; see also Galli, 1981, p. 112).

Chapter 2

The Colonial Legacy in Kenya and Uganda

The colonial period importantly shaped post-independence developments. While Kenya and Uganda both formed part of the East African Protectorate, their colonial experiences diverged in several critical respects:

— how the "central" ethnic groups were treated and behaved;

— how the systems of local rule adopted by the British laid the basis for divisions and government authoritarianism;

— whether a sense of nationhood developed;

— how the very limited economic opportunities permitted for Africans in the colonial period affected post-independence political life;

— how large regional inequalities developed within each country;

— the role and nature of the military;

— religious influences; and

— constitutional settlements devised for independence.

The Kikuyu in Kenya and the Buganda in Uganda felt the most direct effects of colonialism, each being a large group in a fertile area containing the capital. Whereas the colonial authorities advantaged the Buganda, the Kikuyu probably suffered more than the rest of the country.

In Uganda, the colonial government treated the Buganda as privileged, reinforcing existing divisions within the country. The Kingdom of Buganda had a history of at least 400 years. The 1900 Agreement with Buganda, which provided a formal basis for the British Protectorate, gave the Buganda a special role. The colonial authorities viewed them a very superior people, " ... of intelligence and general capacity far beyond any other inhabitants of Central Africa" (Mullins, 1904, p. 17). A colonial law of 1908 awarded land to the Kabaka (the King), his family and major chiefs, in the *mailo* system. In the system of "indirect rule", the British appointed Buganda to administer much of the country outside the Kingdom, while the British and Buganda together attacked neighbouring territory. Buganda received the "lost counties" land taken from Bunyoro. Cash crops were encouraged and education promoted in Buganda and in the South. Westerners and Northerners, lacking economic opportunities in their own territories, came to Buganda as low-paid labourers. The central and privileged role of Buganda, physically and economically, together with the attitudes of the Buganda towards the rest of Uganda and of others towards them — with antecedents in the pre-colonial era but much strengthened by colonial preferences — left a deep fault line in the centre of the Ugandan polity.

In contrast, the Kikuyu, who in 1989 formed 21 per cent of the Kenyan population, received bad treatment in the colonial era, displaced from their land by white settlers. The *Mau Mau* insurgency prior to independence arose largely from this eviction. The system of European commercial agriculture in Kenya depended on contract labour, in particular the so-called squatters, many of them Kikuyu displaced by early British settlement. By the late 1930s, there was general insecurity of tenure and growing landlessness and deteriorating living standards among squatters who had no legally recognised channel to express their interests and very little in the way of the so-called "benefits of colonialism" such as education and other social services. Resistance escalated in response to increasing repression. As one observer put it, the Kikuyu squatter had "very little to lose". Squatter resistance began in the mid-1940s. An oathing campaign, symbolising a unity of purpose, began in late 1947 marking the start of the *Mau Mau* revolt. Europeans in the highlands encountered force against them for the first time in 1950. Grassroots support for *Mau Mau* increased with rising prices (Furedi, 1992, p. 111). The authorities met the *Mau Mau* movement with repressive measures: eviction, seizure of crops and livestock and subjection of the Kikuyu to emergency regulations, including curfew, residence permits and arbitrary arrest. By 1954, when the movement had been effectively repressed, an estimated 15 000 people (the vast majority of whom were Africans) had been killed. The underlying causes of the conflict continued to preoccupy policy makers up to and after independence.

The system of local rule adopted by the British laid the basis for divisions and government authoritarianism. Kenya and Uganda had a shared colonial legacy here, with one critical difference relating to the role of Buganda. The British appointed traditional chiefs to exercise authority at the local level under legislation described as "draconian" (Mugai, 1995). Presented as a development of local customs, the structure in fact perverted them by transforming the constrained authority of traditional chiefs into a more authoritarian, arbitrary and less participatory system (Mamdani, 1996). It undermined traditional authority. The colonial uniforms and helmets of the local authorities symbolised this system designed expressly to "pacify the natives" (Gertzel, 1970). In both countries local administrative boundaries were drawn on ethnic lines, which strengthened ethnic divisions. However in Kenya, local leaders were appointed as administrators through the *Chiefs Act*. In Uganda, Buganda chiefs ruled indirectly not only in Buganda but also in the Northern and Eastern regions, which created long-lasting antagonism.

The colonial period failed to create a sense of nation in the territory that became Uganda, perhaps its most damaging legacy. With the central government viewed as a remote arbiter of disputes, most areas regarded themselves as distinct entities [the *Wallis Report* (1953) noted that each administrative area wanted independence for itself][1]. The Buganda in particular believed that their special, autonomous situation under the Protectorate meant that they would get independent status; they demanded this on several occasions both before and after independence. They refused to participate in the pre-independence legislative council and boycotted the 1961 elections. For many years the colonial authorities themselves were unclear on appropriate boundaries for the country and whether it would form a single state. As Andrew Cohen, a progressive Governor in the 1950s, stated: "It was a [colonial] system which looked at the problems and interests of each given area or tribe. It was not conceived in the framework of building up a state or nation" (Cohen, 1959, pp. 26-27). Obote argued for delay in independence because the less developed areas would be disadvantaged: "We Semi-Hamites and Norsemen of Uganda feel that the Congress in aiming at 'Self-government in Uganda', is hastening and therefore leaving us behind because of our present inability to aim so high" (*Uganda Herald*, 24 April 1952).

Uganda had no equivalent to *Mau Mau*. Political consciousness developed further in Buganda than elsewhere, as it did among the Kikuyu. All the early political movements, protests and organisations came from Buganda — e.g. peasant and worker movements that led to a general strike in 1945 and riots against the British in 1949. Yet Uganda had virtually no *nationalist* movement and no *national* leader. Rushed independence produced a divisive jockeying for power among groups.

Kenya at independence and for some time thereafter had a strong sense of nationhood, with Kenyatta widely perceived as a national leader and, as the first President, frequently referred to as *Meze*, or father. This sense of nation developed despite the divisive form of administration and no common language other than English and limited Swahili. The *Mau Mau* movement played a critical role here in demonstrating the leadership credentials of the Kikuyu to promote local interests against the colonial authorities; resentment against colonial exploitation, fostered by deteriorating economic conditions for Africans in the more densely populated parts of the country and the brutal suppression of *Mau Mau*, was widely shared. Kenyatta became recognised as a national leader largely as a result of his role (including imprisonment) during the *Mau Mau* resistance.

Complete unity did not prevail among the Africans in Kenya. Differences persisted between the Kenyan African Union (KAU)[2], led by Jomo Kenyatta and associated with the Kikuyu and Luo peoples, and the Kenyan African Democratic Union (KADU), led by Daniel arap Moi and affiliated with the Kalinjin and Kamba groups. Yet attainment of independence and the charisma of the first Kenyan president provided sufficient basis for overall national consensus, at least initially. The Kenyan independence experience thus presents a marked contrast to the Ugandan "nation", created by the British and not by the people who lived in it.

Very limited economic opportunities existed for Africans in either country in the colonial era. They were excluded from most activities other than farming up to the 1950s (Brett, 1993). Asians dominated small and medium business. Africans worked mainly in peasant agriculture, petty trade and government. Nonetheless, steps taken by the colonial authorities in the wake of *Mau Mau* did begin to address questions of entitlement and economic opportunities in Kenya. In Uganda control of the state remained virtually the only way to advance, making the acquisition of political power more critical than in countries with more diverse economic opportunities.

Kenya became one of the few African countries that undertook widespread land adjudication and entitlement programmes at an early stage. The authorities saw individual land titles as a solution to the demands that had erupted during *Mau Mau*, as well as a way to improve agricultural production. The British promoted the reform of tenure from a communal system to an individual (freehold) basis in Central province following the Swynnerton Plan in 1954, and this accelerated and expanded after independence. According to a later World Bank report (1983*b*), the Plan did not realise two of its goals — to promote access to credit and help avoid fragmentation of holdings. It did largely fulfil one express objective, however — to create an African commercial class on the land with a vested interest in stability and thereby to contribute to a "politically stable community" (Swynnerton, 1955, p. 10, cited in Hunt, 1996).

Large regional inequalities developed within each country during the colonial period. Development occurred unevenly across the colonies due to bias in the provision of infrastructure and services in favour of the settlers and regions which contributed most to cash crop production. In both countries, but especially in Kenya, cross-cutting cleavages based on class and landholdings began to emerge during the colonial period alongside the racial and regional divide.

In Uganda, significant disparities between the North and South (roughly non-Bantu and Bantu) developed during the colonial period. Development efforts all focused on the South, including education, cash crops, infrastructure and the locus of administration. The North and West were to provide labour for the Centre and South. In 1925, the Director of Agriculture reprimanded a District Officer who had encouraged the growth of cotton in the West Nile, telling him "to refrain from actively stimulating the production of cotton or other economic crops in outlying districts" because the country "is dependent on a supply of labour [from such districts] for the carrying out of essential services in the central or producing areas" (Mamdani, 1976, p. 52). Cotton growing came later in the North, but it remained much less remunerative than the coffee grown in the South.

In Kenya, ethnic and regional inequalities also emerged during the colonial period, but the greatest socio-economic divide was between the African population and the Europeans and Asians. Laws forbade landholding by non-Europeans; other restrictions and subsidies protected European interests. A relatively high poll and hut tax, alongside the prohibition of cultivation of cash crops, forced Africans into squatter contracts and wage labour, helping to bring on the *Mau Mau* rebellion. The colonial

18

alienation of African land and its subsequent division into small African and large non-African farms provided the basis of most current landholding patterns in Kenya, including the continuing dichotomy between large and small farms, particularly in agricultural regions with medium and high potential (World Bank, 1983a). The Swynnerton Plan and subsequent resettlement did not disrupt this colonial pattern.

Kenya had a colonial army which was relatively balanced from an ethnic perspective. In Uganda, however, there was a deliberate policy of ethnic imbalance in the army, which was composed almost entirely of Northerners and Easterners after 1905, when Southerners were told they were too short for service. A theory of "ethnofunctionalism" developed, which held that the people from the North and East were naturally martial; this was still being argued after independence, in statements like "some sections of the population just cannot fight ... even if they are soldiers" (H. Makmot in Republic of Uganda, 1966, vol. 4, p. 755). In general, Northerners had very little education; hence much of the army was illiterate. Very few Ugandan officers had experience or education[3].

In Uganda, competition between foreign missionaries beginning in the nineteenth century and encouraged by the divide-and-rule policy of the Kabaka, left sharp religious divisions. The British favoured the Protestants in access to land and authority, leading to grievances among Catholics and Muslims. Outside religious influences had less obvious divisive effects in Kenya. For much of the period, religious movements were co-opted in the sense that they supported regime stability. More recently, the Council of Churches has vocally advocated multipartyism with peaceful political change.

In both Kenya and Uganda, the constitutions devised for independence sought to entrench regional autonomy and weaken the central government, albeit in different ways, and in both the formulas adopted proved unworkable. The two countries dealt with this in quite different ways. Within two years, the new Kenyan leadership shifted smoothly from a federal to a unitary state. Uganda had a quite peculiar independence constitution. Buganda alone received some autonomy in a federal relationship with the Centre, and the King of Buganda became President of the whole country; other kingdoms had semi-federal status, while the rest of the country was divided into districts of a unitary state. The constitution thus symbolised the stresses that the new country faced, itself embedding a time bomb. It could scarcely endure, while its illogicality justified absence of the respect essential for stable government.

Clearly, each of the elements of the colonial legacy contributed to a potentially explosive mix in Uganda. While the South enjoyed relative wealth, the North dominated the army. Regional and ethnic differences largely coincided with economic inequalities: the Buganda and Southerners had privilege in education and resources; Northern and Eastern areas remained extremely poor and underdeveloped. Religious differences partly coincided and partly cut across these regional, ethnic and economic divisions. Catholics and Protestants were present throughout the country, so that the religious divisions might have acted to counter ethnic ones. Political power offered great rewards, particularly given the few alternative sources of income. With no national unity but ethnically divided groups, securing and sustaining political power became a matter of overwhelming importance.

Despite several similarities with Uganda and the bitter and costly *Mau Mau* conflict, Kenya's colonial legacy created a better basis for future stability in a number of ways. Most notably, perhaps, *Mau Mau* actually had the effect of promoting the desire for independence, establishing the leadership credentials of the Kikuyu and creating a sense of nation. The subsequent redistribution of landholdings widened the section of the population which had an economic interest in stability.

Notes

1. *Wallis Report*, quoted in Mudoola (1992).

2. KAU later became the ruling Kenyan African National Union (KANU) party.

3. Before independence, Amin (himself only semi-literate) beat up a Turkana village community so brutally that he would have been courtmartialed, but this was stopped because he was one of only two African commissioned officers.

Chapter 3

Contrasting Records of Stability and Conflict in Kenya and Uganda

These two countries contrast strongly in political stability and conflict since independence, with Uganda much less stable and experiencing conflict on a much greater scale (Table 3.1). It now has its seventh national leader since independence, whereas Kenya has had only two Presidents, the second the former deputy of the first. This chapter reviews their complex histories in some detail.

Table 3.1. **Violence in Kenya and Uganda: Estimated Deaths**

Period	Kenya			Uganda		
	Events	Deaths		Events	Deaths	
		Total	Homicides and Deaths in Custody		Total	Homicides and Deaths in Custody
1950s	*Mau Mau*	15 000	N/A	- - -	- - -	- - -
1960s	Shifta	3 000	N/A	Riots after referendum on lost counties. Narulabye massacre. Battle of Mengo.	2 500	N/A
1970s	- - -	- - -	920 [a,d]	Amin terror, 1971-79, especially against Acholi and Langi	over 300 000	N/A
1980s	- - -	- - -	1 410 [b,d]	1979 attack on West Nile. 1984-85 massacre of Buganda in Luwero Triangle	300 000 to 500 000	N/A
1990s	Ethnic clashes, Rift Valley (1994-95). Mob violence	1 500	2 000 [c,d]	1986-96 rebellions in North and West	3 000 to 5 000	1 720 [d,e]
Total (est.)		19 692	1 780 [d]		605 500 to 807 500	1 720 [d]

Notes: *a)* based on two years; *b)* based on one year; *c)* estimate includes 819 deaths in custody, 1994-95; *d)* estimate of annual average (see other notes); *e)* 1991-94 average.

Sources: Kenya Human Rights Commission (1995); Africa Watch (1993); Sivard (1993); Republic of Kenya (1981, 1985).

Uganda

Political violence has marked each of the four periods of Ugandan post-independence political history — Obote's first period in power, 1962-71 (Obote I); the Amin era (1971-79); transition then Obote's second regime, 1980-85 (Obote II); and transition then Museveni's rule (since 1986). Hindsight shows the Obote I era as relatively peaceful, except when the Kabaka was deposed in 1966 and an estimated 2 000 people were killed. State-inspired violence characterised the Idi Amin era, culminating in invasion by a combined Tanzanian and Ugandan-rebel force in 1978 which overthrew the regime. The Amin era saw over 300 000 killed, mainly by government troops. Violence at least as bad stamped the second Obote regime, however, as the army wrought uncontrolled havoc, especially in the Luwero Triangle of Buganda where rebel forces were active; some 300 000-500 000 people died violently. Many more deaths occurred indirectly over these 15 years as economic decline, worsening food production and the disintegration of health services led to rising mortality. Museveni, who led the successful rebels to power in 1986, has faced rebellions in the North and the Northwest, with deaths over the last decade estimated to be at least 5 000.

Obote I: 1962-71

Milton Obote came to power initially in coalition with the Buganda. The moment he could manage without them he centralised control and sought to marginalise them. Two particular events alienated this group. In 1964, his referendum over the "lost counties", land taken from Bunyoro during the Protectorate and allocated to Buganda, gave the land back to Bunyoro; this led to riots in Buganda, harshly suppressed with a number of deaths. Then, in 1966, Obote suspended the Constitution, assumed the presidency, displaced the Kabaka, and denied Buganda its semi-federal status. When King Mutesa (the Kabaka), the constitutional President of Uganda, appealed for international assistance and Buganda's parliament passed a resolution demanding secession (Karugire, 1980), government troops led by Idi Amin attacked the King's palace in the battle of Mengo, the first major bloodbath in independent Uganda. An estimated 2 000 died, including many civilians. This incident showed Obote's readiness to sacrifice constitutional law and use armed force against civilians, if necessary, to sustain his power. It earned him the implacable hatred of the Buganda.

In 1964, army mutinies occurred throughout East Africa. Kenya responded by increasing political control over its military[1], but Obote reacted by significantly raising pay, purchasing equipment and promoting officers. Larger, better armed and with a newly created air force, the Ugandan army gained more power, particularly after its successful involvement in the Congo rebellion. Obote relied increasingly on it, purging its Bantu officers in 1965.

Obote became increasingly authoritarian, alienating many groups by abuses of human rights and promotion of his own people while relying on the army for support. The state of emergency declared in Buganda early in 1966 was extended to other parts of the country in 1969. From 1969, he proscribed political parties and proposed that the presidency should be his for life. He aimed to restore his popularity with his "Move to the Left" and "People's Charter", but he had permanently alienated the Buganda, annoyed the Catholics by discriminatory education policies, and offended prominent Protestants and Muslims in various ways (Mudoola, 1992). Political and religious leaders suffered arrests and many in the middle class — businessmen, lawyers, teachers, doctors — as well as people from other walks of life faced detention from time to time. Nonetheless, state-sponsored violence during these years was modest compared with later developments.

The army, loyal to Obote in 1966, divided into an Amin faction (Nilotic as was Amin), and an Obote group composed mainly of Acholis and Langis. Disputes between Obote and Amin increased. The Amin coup occurred during Obote's visit to Singapore in January 1971 for a conference of Commonwealth leaders. In a mistake of Shakespearean proportions, Obote had told Amin before leaving that he was to be investigated for embezzlement and murder on Obote's return.

The Amin Regime: 1971-79

The Amin coup caused initial jubilation among the many groups Obote had alienated, but slaughter of civilians and soldiers soon began, at first mostly Acholi and Langi; then Amin initiated his "economic war", expelling Asians, citizens and non-citizens; violence then extended to anyone suspected of challenging him. The Acholis and Langis, Obote supporters, dominated the army and gave Amin a strong sense of insecurity. He used abortive coups as the excuse to attempt to purge them, with massive killings[2]. Expulsion of certain groups of foreign nationals followed — all Israelis on the grounds of sabotage, followed by 50 000 Asians who together owned and controlled perhaps half of the country's wealth. Amin described this as "part of an 'Economic War' [intended] to make an ordinary Ugandan master of his own economic destiny"[3]. Asian assets went to Amin's followers, chiefly from his own (Nubian) tribe. In December 1972, the "Economic War" extended to British interests when the government took over all tea estates and a number of British companies.

The powers of the military police increased greatly. A 1973 decree empowered them to arrest people without a court order or an arrest warrant, on the basis of suspicion alone (Bwengye, 1985). After attempted coups in 1973 and 1974, Amin reorganised the army, bringing it directly under his control. He created a Defence Council which encroached on the duties of the Cabinet. In effect, Amin moulded the army into a state instrument for the consolidation of his personal power. It increasingly replaced the police in effecting arrests. Violence and murder became institutionalised. Disappearances and summary executions grew common, some performed in public. Many prominent people were killed in the chaos. Dragged from his chambers in broad daylight, the Chief Justice, Ben Kiwanuka, disappeared. The independence of the judiciary and the rule of law had been destroyed. Many, particularly among the well-educated middle class, fled to other countries if they could.

In October 1978, Amin invaded Northwestern Tanzania, claiming it as part of Uganda. The Tanzanian People's Defence Forces, together with Ugandan opposition groups that formed the Uganda National Liberation Front (UNLF), attacked central and western Uganda and defeated the Amin army.

The Day of the Uganda National Liberation Front (UNLF): 1979-80

The forces which overthrew Amin contained a variety of groups with different ideologies and aspirations, whose only common goal had been to remove Amin[4]. The Tanzanians remained powerful behind the scenes, retaining a sizeable military force in the country. A Military Commission was formed to take political decisions. In the next two years, three administrations held office as rival groups jockeyed for power — Professor Yusuf Lule, a Buganda, briefly became President but alienated powerful forces, partly because of plans to reform the military. After only two months Godfrey Binaisa QC, one of Obote's right-hand men in the early 1960s, replaced him. Corruption and confusion marked his regime and in May 1980 the pro-Obote UNLF forces removed him. Throughout, the Tanzanians appeared determined to re-establish Obote in power.

During this confusion, Acholi and Langi soldiers in the Uganda National Liberation Army (UNLA) proceeded to revenge the massacres of Amin. Indiscriminate killings in West Nile, Idi Amin's home area, destroyed most of the town of Arua. According to the UN High Commission for Refugees, over a quarter of a million refugees from West Nile fled to neighbouring countries like Sudan and Zaire (Karugire, 1980).

The general election which followed Binaisa's overthrow was contested by the traditional political parties — the Protestant and anti-Buganda Uganda People's Congress (UPC) led by Obote, and the Catholic and Buganda Democratic Party (DP) — as well as the new Uganda Patriotic Movement (UPM), led by Yoweri Museveni. The election was rigged, however. Although it appears clear that the DP won the majority of votes, the Military Commission declared Milton Obote the winner[5].

Obote II: 1980-85

Milton Obote was sworn in to his second presidency in December 1980. In the face of election fraud and "… the system of institutionalised violence unleashed upon the people of Uganda"[6], the National Resistance Army (NRA), led by Museveni, along with some other opposition groups, launched an armed struggle against the government. The NRA established itself in parts of central Uganda, particularly in the region immediately surrounding the capital known as the "Luwero Triangle". Most of the NRA were Buganda, because the Obote army had particularly victimised them. Museveni himself came from Ankole.

The government responded brutally, not discriminating between the guerrillas — elusive and not often captured — and civilians, who were arbitrarily detained, tortured, raped and killed. Conservative estimates are that about 300 000 people may have been killed during these years and another 500 000 displaced in Buganda alone (Mutibwa, 1992). Many commentators suggest that the extent of human rights abuse under Obote II exceeded that in the Amin years.

By mid-1985, the lack of military success against the rebels had undermined the regime. Soldiers, especially Acholis whom the NRA killed in large numbers, decided to negotiate. Obote's support even within the UNLA dwindled, partly because he refused to negotiate and partly because he promoted Langis above Acholis. The UNLA replaced him with a military council headed by Major-General Tito Okello. The security situation in Kampala continued to deteriorate, with rival armed bands controlling different parts of the city, while mass killings continued in the Luwero Triangle. Meanwhile, the Museveni rebels took advantage of the chaos in the UNLA to consolidate their control over the rural areas of Southwest Uganda and to capture military garrisons in the major towns to the west of Kampala. The NRA proceeded with the war until they captured Kampala in January 1986, and Yoweri Museveni became President.

Museveni: 1986-96

Museveni appointed a government broad-based politically and ethnically, although recently it has been accused of giving Ankole disproportionate jobs and influence. Prominent members of the various political parties and the different regions and religions in the country gained positions in the administration, even if the balance favoured the Western and Central regions. When it came to power, the National Resistance Movement (NRM) government described itself as an interim administration, announcing a four-year timetable for drawing up a new constitution and holding elections. In late 1989, however, it extended itself for a further five years. The regime sought to maintain a monopoly on organised political activity; political parties such as the DP and UPC could exist but could not organise activities such as public meetings. A presidential election — without political parties — finally came in March 1996, with an easy victory for Museveni.

The regime aimed to incorporate all the various military forces into a single national army (the NRA), with a balanced ethnic composition (Mudoola, 1988). This included not only the various forces that had fought against Obote, but also the UNLF and later Amin supporters from the West Nile. Soldiers who had served in the Obote army went to camps for screening and "political education". This policy expanded the NRA from a small, tightly disciplined guerrilla force into one of the largest armies in Africa, more than 100 000 strong.

Within months of coming to power the Museveni government faced armed opposition in the West Nile, the North and Northeast from supporters of Amin and Obote. West Nile, Amin's area, had been ferociously attacked in 1979, causing a flight to Zaire. Moses Ari, a former Amin minister, led armed opposition from this group but soon surrendered and received a government position. Armed opposition of fluctuating strength has continued in the West with support from Zaire and Sudan.

To combat armed opposition in the North, the NRM government combined negotiations with military action. It announced an amnesty for those who surrendered. It integrated rebels reporting to the authorities into the NRA or sent them to rehabilitation camps for political and vocational training; many returned to civilian life. By late 1986, at least two insurgent groups operated in the North and Northeastern areas inhabited by the Acholi — the Uganda People's Democratic Army (UPDA) and the Holy Spirit Movement. A peace agreement was reached with a substantial part of the UPDA in April 1988. The rest combined with the Holy Spirit Movement under the leadership of Joseph Kony. In early 1991, following further surrenders, those remaining in violent opposition renamed themselves the United Democratic Christian Army (UDCA). This Northern insurgency has continued, at varying levels of ferocity, with support from the Sudanese government and with deliberate and arbitrary killings of hundreds of people. Some of the victims have been elected members of Resistance Committees (organs of local government, instituted by Museveni), but most have been ordinary villagers with no institutional connection to the government. Civilians have been abducted and forced to stay with the rebels, sometimes forcibly recruited as new fighters. Mutilation has been widely used to punish civilians suspected of co-operating with the authorities (Amnesty International, 1992). The NRA has responded with violence against civilians as well as the guerrillas in villages alleged to support the rebels.

Violence thus persists in the North and West of Uganda. In both cases, it intertwines with the situations in neighbouring countries; in the North the Sudanese support the rebels, while the Ugandan government supports opposition forces in Sudan. In the West, Ugandan government forces supported the Zairian rebels and the Zairian government the anti-Museveni forces. Violence has, nonetheless, persisted even after the successful ousting of Mobutu.

Kenya

Mass violence has not stained Kenya's post-independence history as it has marked Uganda's. Yet Kenya has had episodes of conflict since the 1950s, as summarised in Table 3.1. It has taken various forms: state-sponsored; group conflict encompassing civil strife which may or may not be state-sponsored; and serious interpersonal violence. The major violent movements include *Mau Mau* (already covered above as part of the colonial legacy), the Shifta wars and ethnic clashes in the Rift Valley and Western province, as well as growing criminality.

The attainment of independence and the charisma of the first President appeared to provide sufficient basis for overall consensus, at least initially. The first Development Plan set out Kenyan "African Socialism" in terms of "political democracy, social welfare, a mixed economy and self-reliance, including gradual Africanisation of assets and jobs" (Berg-Schlosser and Siegler, 1990, p. 14). Political power steadily centralised in the Office of the President during the Kenyatta era, with the new (1966) constitution and subsequent legislation. The *Preservation of Public Security Act* permitted detention without trial, and a one-party system became the *de facto* rule.

The Kenyatta government strengthened its control through threatened and actual coercion as well as rewards. It acted harshly against perceived opponents through detention and banning (e.g. of Oginga Odinga, and the avowedly socialist Kenya People's Union), and allegedly had involvement in political assassinations of potential rivals to Kenyatta — including Pinto (1965), Mboya (1969) and Kariuki (1975). A diverse array of patronage rewards served *inter alia* to heal the divisions among the Kikuyu and to promote stability. The Kenyatta period saw the growth of Kikuyu economic and political dominance, and Central province prospered. Indeed contemporary media reports refer to a sentiment among the "peripheral" groups that the process of Kenyanisation was really one of "Kikuyu-isation". Corruption — e.g. in granting licences and procurement contracts — reportedly became endemic in government.

Nonetheless, the overall system of state patronage and its rewards in Kenya incorporated the leaders of virtually all ethnic groups (with the exception of the Luo after 1966) (Throup, 1996). Electoral competition at the local level appeared vibrant, amidst regular elections to the National Assembly. Critics of the Kenyatta regime (such as the Law Society and the churches) could express their opinions and parliamentary critics were often elected. Indeed, in 1969 and 1974 only about one-quarter of the parliamentary backbenchers were re-elected. "Political life remained remarkably open and its press comparatively free by African standards" (Throup, 1996, p. 72). Provided that one remained within the party (which itself did not entail any strict ideological constraints) and did not criticise the President, an individual politician had considerable freedom. Observers have noted that the regime managed to be responsive without democratic representation and that the semi-competitive regular elections helped to diffuse potential conflict.

The only systematic organised violence arose in the Shifta wars in the 1960s, when the people of the North, who had voted in a referendum in the early 1960s to secede and join Somalia, took up arms against the state. The region has a long history of conflicts among its people, fought mainly over territory (water and pasture), livestock raids, assertion of dominance and retribution. To some extent, such conflicts have prevailed up to the present day. The Shifta wars lasted until 1968, under a loose, exiled leadership based in Somalia and the Middle East. The conflict itself became a desert guerrilla campaign against the symbols of central authority. The government relied on punitive and repressive measures which provided extraordinary powers to enter homes, search them, seize property and detain, and in certain proscribed areas, shoot people on sight, destroy any building and seize or destroy livestock. The original unity among the secessionists gradually broke down, while the Shifta continued to raid villages, kill and loot. The Kenyan authorities' approach became increasingly

27

indiscriminate, with collective punishment in response to incidents of banditry and poaching (Sora, 1995). A period of relative calm followed a peace agreement between the Somali and Kenyan heads of state in 1968; it lasted through the eruption of the Ogaden war between Somalia and Ethiopia.

Upon the death of the first President, his deputy, Moi, took temporary and then longer-term control of the country. Coming from the "periphery" (Tugen/Kalenjin), he faced fierce resistance from the Kikuyu establishment which perceived its privileged position as under threat. In fact the early Moi years produced a series of populist measures that sought to appeal to the poorer elements in Kenyan society, tending to bypass the established patrons. This undermined potential competitors in the political arena. Moi sought to broaden the base of development in Kenya and benefit his allies in the Rift Valley, Western and Coast provinces.

The prominence of Kikuyu in government and the civil service gradually waned during the Moi period. Most of the elite managed to adapt to the new order, however, and continued in business and parliamentary life. In 1982, a spectacular but unsuccessful coup attempt by the Kikuyu-dominated air force, supported by university students, shook the regime. The President thereafter moved to exclude Kikuyu systematically from positions of influence within the government (Nelson, 1986), and became increasingly repressive over the 1980s. The state formally became a one-party regime through constitutional amendment. More importantly, the ruling party (KANU) was revived, and Kalenjin and Luyha interests promoted therein[7]. Party membership became a virtual prerequisite for civil service advancement, access to loans and so on (Throup, 1996, Chapter 3). Resort to detentions without trial and repression of union and other potential opposition continued (Holmquist, Weaver and Ford, 1994). The press began to exercise greater self-censorship. Finally and perhaps most significantly, the judgement that people had been able to pass on their representatives through the electoral process was undermined. Even without substantive policy choices, regular elections had linked the decision-making elite to mass expectations and rewarded their ability to deliver. Systematic rigging escalated, however, and in 1986 the new system of queue voting (replacing the secret ballot) greatly facilitated voter intimidation.

In the early 1990s, domestic and international pressures for political liberalisation grew, culminating in the suspension of aid in 1991. In response, President Moi acceded to multiparty elections and greatly relaxed media controls. The initially unified opposition, under the banner of the Forum for Restoration of Democracy (FORD), suffered what proved an irretrievable breakdown. Three main parties and five much smaller ones emerged to oppose KANU. During the presidential campaign, Moi relied on the security forces and the Provincial Administration for surveillance and disruption of the opposition. Most notoriously, his political tactics extended to direct sponsorship of the ethnic clashes of 1992 (Africa Watch, 1993). They served to create a sense of insecurity so that voters would prefer the certainty associated with the status quo (KANU), and to change the ethnic balance in the Rift Valley, a crucial area in electoral terms (it accounted for 44 of the 183 seats).

The election did not provide an overwhelming or even majority endorsement of the President. Yet with 36.5 per cent of the vote Moi still obtained the largest share in the face of the divided opposition. The results clearly demonstrated the significance of local and ethnic loyalties (Mugai, 1995, p. 190). The Moi and KANU strongholds emerged in the Coast (a former KADU stronghold, where Moi got 62 per cent of the vote), and the Northeastern (62 per cent) provinces. In Nairobi, dominated by Kikuyu whose home districts neighbour the city, Moi received only 16 per cent of the vote, in Eastern province only 2 per cent and in Nyanza, home of the Luo, only 14 per cent. In the Rift Valley, where ethnic clashes had displaced tens if not hundreds of thousands of voters, Moi received 66 per cent. In the National Assembly, KANU has no elected Kikuyu or Luo parliamentarians or ministers. In 1996, all the elected Kikuyu and Luo sat on the opposition benches.

A number of occasions of civil strife have occurred during the Moi period. For example in 1982 — following the coup attempt — two days of rampage and looting erupted in Nairobi, directed especially at the Asian community. Reports of the Kenya Human Rights Commission and Africa Watch suggest that significant episodes of violence in the larger urban areas are not uncommon. In the 1990s, the "ethnic clashes" in the Rift Valley and Western province claimed 1 500 deaths, with at least 300 000 displaced, homes and granaries burnt, crops destroyed just prior to harvest, property looted and livestock stolen. The primary aggressors were male youth, known as "Kalenjin warriors". The government portrayed the clashes as fulfilment of the forecast repercussions of multipartyism. Several other detailed studies, including those of a parliamentary committee of the (then) KANU-only National Assembly, the National Council of Churches of Kenya (NCCK) and Africa Watch, closely implicated the regime in the clashes. Senior government figures allegedly promoted violence directly through sponsorship of private armies and inflammatory public statements.

The domestic security apparatus proved unwilling to control the violence or arrest the perpetrators. The clashes had a clear ethnic dimension; but the violence was directed against the smallholder Kikuyu and large farmers were left relatively unscathed. In addition to such events as the Molo massacre in 1992, the press reports from the period suggest that much of the violence took place on a continuing, small-scale basis; for example, in Mount Elgon in mid-June five people died in a series of attacks over as many days (*The Standard*, 19 June 1992). Violent incidents sharing similar features continued in 1996. Insecurity prevails among the displaced; many have not returned to their former homes and some remain in refugee camps.

Up to the mid-1990s, attacks on government agents represented the most dramatic form of insecurity in the Northeast, although these incidents remained much less common than attacks on convoys, the main form of transport in the region. Heavily armed bands raiding villages and livestock cause less publicised but pervasive terror (Maalim, 1995). In Northeastern province, reports suggest the emergence of unsupervised private armies and the effective abdication of power by government (Umar, 1995, p. 68). Large tracts reportedly have become "no-go" areas. Some local leaders have supported the bandits. Historical animosities between government security agencies and local communities have contributed to the agencies' abdication of responsibility for protection of life and property in the communities.

The situation in Kenya became tense again in 1997, with numerous outbreaks of violence in major cities and especially on the coast. Distinct types of conflict appeared: clashes between opposition supporters and authorities (police) in Nairobi and on university campuses, and more general outbreaks of conflict which typically involved gangs, destruction of personal property and displacement as well as deaths, having sharper economic overtones. Some observers argue that the two types of violence are intimately related and that, as before, the government was implicated in provoking ethnic clashes.

Violent conflict escalated on the coast around Mombasa in mid-1997, echoing the pattern in the Rift Valley in the early 1990s, with reports of gangs descending upon groups of displaced people who had taken refuge in places such as churches. In one such incident on 22 August, two people were killed. Gang violence directed against the authorities also appeared, with reports of police deaths. In another reported incident, 150 armed men attacked a police control point just north of Mombasa. The overall death toll on the coast reached at least 40 by the end of August 1997. Homes and stalls were set ablaze. Reports suggested linkage of the violence to a group that sought to exclude "outsiders" from the Coastal region and keep land for local people. Many of the Kenyan dead came originally from outside the region (*Financial Times*, 20 August 1997). As before, the President and government denounced the violence as "tribalism".

Opposition agitation revolved around the electoral laws, claimed to favour the incumbent President. Pressure for reform mounted in advance of the general election. An escalating pro-reform campaign at several points degenerated into violence and deaths. In early July, 14 people were killed when police violently broke up rallies called by the reform lobby across the country, on the anniversary of the rally for multiparty politics five years before when police forcefully dispersed crowds, leaving 28 dead. The government closed two public universities and a polytechnic in Nairobi as a result of the July riots. Just a few miles from State House in the capital students marched chanting "Moi-butu, Moi-butu out!" (*Africa Confidential*, Volume 38, No. 24). The police attacks extended to beating clergy with truncheons in churches associated with the opposition.

The opposition nevertheless remained fragmented, with no agreed single candidate to oppose the President in the 1997 election. Strikes called in August 1997 had effect only in Nairobi and parts of Central province and did not have undivided opposition support. Nonetheless, more political coherence appeared behind demands for constitutional and electoral reform.

Churches, non-governmental organisations, foreign missions and a number of western foreign ministries denounced strong-arm methods of breaking up opposition rallies — on top of more general pressure for democratic reform. The United States, for example, expressly set out conditions to be met for the forthcoming general elections. The IMF withdrew its support on 31 July 1997, on the grounds of continued corruption. It withheld further disbursement from its $220 million balance-of-payments support pending measures to curb government corruption — an unprecedented action when fiscal and monetary targets were broadly in line.

National elections were held in Kenya at the end of 1997. Despite widespread allegations of vote rigging and intimidation of opposition candidates, Moi once again retained power with a little over 40 per cent of the vote. It seems that there will not be a change at the helm until the next century when Moi will have no alternative but to retire gracefully.

Following the 1997 election, the apparent proneness of Kenya to violence looks set to continue. Crime in various forms, even if not within the strict ambit of "group conflict", remains a significant and perhaps the key dimension of tension and conflict in contemporary Kenya, in both urban and rural areas. Table 3.1 includes trends in homicides committed since the early 1970s. Although not approaching the scale seen in neighbouring Uganda, gang attacks on individuals and their homes and property create pervasive insecurity among the threatened groups. While the conflict has overt ethnic tones, it also has important economic roots associated with increasing disparities and the slowdown in the growth of opportunities for youth.

Notes

1. In Kenya, the army was kept small, and firmly under political control; Tanzania converted its army into a people's militia.

2. The first killings came after an attempted coup in July 1971, when Acholi and Langi soldiers were massacred at Ganga, Maratha and Mbarara barracks; the second occurred at Mutukula on the Uganda-Tanzania border in February 1972; the third arose from another attempted coup in June 1972; and the fourth coincided with the departure of the Asians, also in June 1972.

3. Amin's speech to university students in 1972.

4. The Chairman was Paulo Muwanga, a veteran UPC politician supported by the Tanzanians.

5. The early results strongly favoured the DP, whereupon Muwanga announced that all further results would be declared by the Military Commission; a decree was issued that anyone who talked about the results would be subject to imprisonment. The UPC and Obote were then declared the winners (Mudoola, 1988).

6.   Museveni, quoted in Mutibwa (1992), p. 155.

7.   Specifically, political patronage concentrated on the Tugen and Keiyo rather than the Nandi group within the Kalenjin.

Chapter 4

Economic and Social Factors Relevant to Conflict in Kenya and Uganda

Economic and Social Policies and Performance

Although both countries have sometimes faced serious macroeconomic difficulties, Kenya has clearly outperformed Uganda over most of the post-independence period — and particularly so from 1970 to the mid-1980s. Moreover, the people of Kenya witnessed steady improvements in most social indicators, while in Uganda many of the indicators fell back during the 1970s. Kenya also leads in several other dimensions of performance, including domestic revenue and indicators of confidence such as foreign investment.

The Post-Independence Booms

Both economies did well during the initial decade or so after independence, with GDP growing at a rate of about 6 per cent a year and only moderate inflation. Consumption per head grew faster in Uganda, while Kenya devoted more resources to investment (Table 4.1).

Both governments pursued an import substitution strategy for industrial development through customs duties and import licences, with success manifested in rapid industrial growth. At the same time, the external sector played an important role with continued access to East African markets and foreign direct investment (FDI), for which policies maintained a favourable climate. In Kenya guaranteed profit repatriation (through, for example, the *Foreign Investment Protection Act, 1964*) and tax benefits helped attract FDI. Despite numerous controls on pricing and economic activity in Kenya and an expanding parastatal sector, principles of private ownership and enterprise remained fairly well entrenched during the first decade. Obote initially followed similar policies, but "moved to the left" in the later years of his first regime, nationalising some industries.

Table 4.1. **Macroeconomic Performance in Kenya, Uganda and Tanzania**

(Growth and inflation in per cent per year; investment/GDP in per cent)

Period	Country	GDP Growth	Per Capita GDP Growth	Growth of Private Consumption	Inflation	Investment to GDP Ratio
1960s	Uganda	6.0 [a]	2.3 [a]	5.6	2.4 [a]	11 [b]
	Kenya	6.2 [c]	2.8 [c]	2.9	2.7 [c]	14
	Tanzania	6.0	2.3	6.6	1.6	14 [d]
1970s	Uganda	-1.2	-4.1	-4.0	47.4 [e]	6 [f]
	Kenya	4.4 [g]	0.4 [g]	5.9	10.1 [e]	25
	Tanzania	3.7	-0.2	6.5	11.9	29
1980s	Uganda	3.1	0.2	2.9	92.7	12 [h]
	Kenya	4.2	0.5	4.7	11.8	25
	Tanzania	2.3	-0.8	3.3	31.0	21
1990-95	Uganda	6.6	4.0	6.4	19.7	161
	Kenya	1.4	-2.6	4.5	27.2	19
	Tanzania	4.3 [i]	1.4 [j]	N/A	27.3	32

Notes: a) 1962-71; b) 1965; c) 1964-72; d) 1960; e) 1970-82; f) 1980; g) 1972-81; h) 1987; i) 1993-95; j) 1990-94.

Sources: World Bank, *World Development Report* (various editions); World Bank (1997); World Bank files; Bank of Tanzania.

In Kenya the immediate post-independence period saw extensive efforts by the new government to overcome various elements of the prevalent strong racial bias. Most visibly, a process of land redistribution transferred 1.9 million acres of former European land to African ownership during the first decade. At the same time, Africans replaced Europeans in industry and government through the "Africanisation" policies. Both measures increased the African stake in economic prosperity. Uganda needed less radical measures because of the smaller role of Europeans in the economy.

In both economies, employment expanded significantly in the early years — the numbers employed in the civil service in Kenya grew at 10 per cent annually in the 1970s (four times faster than formal employment in the private sector; World Bank, 1988). In Uganda, total African employment grew by nearly 40 per cent from 1962 to 1970.

In Kenya, the share of government in GDP tripled between 1964 and 1972, while that of parastatals rose five times. Kenya developed a relatively diversified and effective tax base. The share of taxation in GDP rose from 12 per cent in 1966 to 18 per cent by 1972, helping to finance the expansion of public programmes. Uganda's revenue share was lower (14 per cent in 1972), but government expenditure accounted for a very similar slice of national income in both countries in 1972 — 22 per cent in Uganda and 21 per cent in Kenya (Table 4.2).

Table 4.2. **Government Revenue and Expenditure, Uganda, Kenya and Tanzania**

Year	Per Cent of GDP						Per Cent of Total Government Expenditure								
	Revenue			Expenditure			Social Expenditure			Defence Expenditure			Social Expenditure		
	U	K	T	U	K	T	U	K	T	U	K	T	U	K	T
1972	13.7	18.0	15.8	21.8	21.0	19.7	4.5	6.3	4.8	23.1	6.0	11.9	20.6	29.8	24.5
1981	0.7	23.5	11.9	3.2	28.4	21.2	0.5	8.1	2.4	34.5	10.7	11.2	14.9	28.4	17.6
1990	7.4	22.4	15.3	14.6	28.1	17.3	2.2 [a]	7.1	4.0	26.9 [a]	10.0	17.3	16.7 [a]	25.3	24.8
1994	8.2	23.5	N/A	18.4	29.9	N/A		7.2	N/A		6.2	N/A		24.2	N/A

Note: a) 1987.
Sources: World Bank, *World Development Report* (various editions) and world data set.

Social expenditure (health and education) formed a significantly higher proportion of total government expenditure in Kenya than in Uganda by 1972, partly because Uganda spent much more on defence as a result of Obote's expansion of the army (Table 4.2). Nonetheless, both countries achieved significant expansion in education and health services, and social indicators showed important improvements (Table 4.3). Education grew massively in Kenya during the first years after independence as the government sought to overcome historical racial disadvantage and meet popular aspirations. Between 1964 and 1968, total primary enrolments rose by over 5 per cent annually, and secondary enrolments by 30 per cent. The number of secondary schools surged from 101 to 601, and the number of secondary students from 27 509 to 101 361. Education, especially secondary education, developed less dramatically in Uganda, but that country had a proportionately larger increase in doctor availability. Both countries saw a significant fall in infant mortality rates.

The 1970s and the Amin Era

The two countries' aggregate economic and social performance diverged sharply in the 1970s. Kenya continued to show improvements on most fronts, although at a somewhat slower rate, but Amin's misrule led to declining GDP, a collapse in government revenue and expenditure, and accelerating inflation. Uganda suffered significant economic regression during Amin's rule — both from the disruption and uncertainty associated with the brutal policies of the regime and from the "economic war" against the Asians, the Israelis and the British. From 1971 to 1980, monetary GDP fell by 3.6 per cent annually and non-monetary output by an estimated 0.8 per cent. Estimated per capita income in 1980 hit only 60 per cent of its 1971 level, whereas Kenya's had increased by about 5 per cent. Manufacturing suffered especially; the share of industry in monetary GDP plummeted to 4.3 per cent from 8.5 per cent. Tax revenues collapsed and expenditures were diverted to the military from the productive and social sectors. Medical and education services deteriorated badly. Population per doctor almost doubled to 27 600 in 1977; medical facilities were destroyed, and outpatient attendance at hospitals fell by half (Dodge and Weibe, 1985). Health indicators, including infant mortality rates, worsened. Primary and secondary enrolment rates slumped in the latter part of the 1970s. Daily calorie supply plunged to 1 778 (amongst the lowest in the world) in 1981 from 2 383 in 1965 (Table 4.3).

Table 4.3. **Social Developments in Kenya, Uganda and Tanzania**

	1960	1970	1980	1990	1995
Calories per Person					
Uganda	2 383[a]	2 096[b]	1 778[c]	2 180[d]	N/A
Kenya	2 289[a]	2 117[b]	2 056	2 075[e]	N/A
Tanzania	1 832[a]	2 003[b]	2 310	2 021[e]	N/A
Calories as Percentage of Requirements					
Uganda	96[a]	90	80	93[d]	N/A
Kenya	98[a]	91	88	89[f]	N/A
Tanzania	85[a]	86[b]	83	94	N/A
Primary School Enrolments (per cent)					
Uganda	49	54[b]	50	67	91[g]
Kenya	48	58	110	95[h]	91[g]
Tanzania	25	34	93	70	70[g]
Secondary School Enrolment [o] (per cent)					
Uganda	3	4	5	11[g]	13[n]
Kenya	2	9	19	23[h]	25[n]
Tanzania	2	3	3	5	5[g]
Population per Doctor (thousands)					
Uganda	15.0	9.2	26.0	21.7[i]	N/A
Kenya	10.7	8.0	7.9	10.1	N/A
Tanzania	21.0	22.9	17.6	28.3[j]	N/A
Population with Access to Safe Water (per cent)					
Uganda	N/A	35[k]	16[l]	34[m]	42
Kenya	N/A	17[k]	28	53[m]	43
Tanzania	N/A	39[k]	46[l]	52	49
Adult Literacy (per cent)					
Uganda	25	44	43[l]	54[g]	61[e]
Kenya	20	32	47	69	77[e]
Tanzania	10	66[k]	79	74[n]	N/A
Infant Mortality Rate (per 1 000 live births)					
Uganda	133	117	113	114[f]	98
Kenya	112	102	83	61[f]	58
Tanzania	144	132	119	87	82

Notes: a) 1965; b) 1974; c) 1981; d) 1988-90; e) 1994; f) 1993; g) 1991; h) 1992; i) 1989-90; j) 1985; k) 1975; l) 1983; m) 1990-95; n) 1993. o) Enrolment rates can exceed 100 because children outside the age cohort covered may attend school.

Sources: UNDP (1996) and *Human Development Report* (various editions); World Bank (1989, 1996a) and *World Development Report* (various editions).

Kenya suffered a series of external shocks which slowed economic growth, but most indicators continued nonetheless to improve. Kenya's fairly open economy — up to a third of output was exported, and about 30 per cent imported — was seriously affected by the oil price rises of 1973 and 1979, the break-up of the East African Community in 1976 and the drought of 1979-80. The overall economic policy stance remained much as in the period following independence and the emphasis on expansion of social services continued. Economic growth slowed but per capita growth remained positive, with rising per capita consumption (over 2 per cent a year). Investment amounted to a quarter of GNP in 1980 (compared with just 6 per cent in Uganda), revenue and expenditure rose as a proportion of GDP and the share of social outlays remained at nearly 30 per cent of government expenditure. Consequently, while health and education expenditure fell to just half a percentage point of GDP in Uganda by 1981, it rose to over 8 per cent in Kenya. In 1974, the Kenyan government eliminated fees for the first four primary grades. President Moi's first development plan (1979-84) set out the overall goal of poverty alleviation and aimed, among other things, to improve the provision of basic needs. A free milk programme was introduced in primary schools in 1979, for example. Social indicators continued to advance, with very substantial increases in primary and secondary enrolment and in access to safe water. Education's share in GDP rose to 6.1 per cent in 1976 from 3.4 per cent at independence. Net primary enrolment reached 86 per cent from only 50 per cent at independence. The average distance of rural households to water nearly halved over the decade to 1984, from 3.4 km. to 1.8 km. The infant mortality rate improved by 20 per cent between 1970 and 1980.

Post-1980: Confusion then Recovery in Uganda; Debt and Adjustment in Kenya

Economic performance diverged after 1980 as well, but less sharply. Uganda had some initial recovery, followed by further deterioration during the widespread conflict towards the end of the second Obote regime. Since 1986, it has seen sustained recovery from a very low base. Kenya has wrestled with the debt, foreign exchange and adjustment crisis that beset most of Africa. The early 1980s were years of economic hardship throughout Africa. The accumulated debt, resulting mainly from borrowing to finance higher-priced oil plus global recession in the early 1980s and worsening commodity prices, contributed to foreign exchange shortages. Kenya's current account deficit mounted relative to GDP and annual inflation rose to average almost 13 per cent compared to less than 3 per cent in the decade before. Kenyan growth averaged 2.7 per cent over 1980-85. It recovered to a healthy 5 per cent between 1986 and 1990, boosted by a short-lived coffee boom, but then fell to 2.3 per cent in 1991 and 0.2 per cent in 1992. The average for 1989-94 was below 1.5 per cent. Per capita income in 1994 stood at only $250, almost 40 per cent less than in 1980. Inflationary pressures remained high. The Consumer Price Index jumped by almost 19 per cent annually from 1980 and over 30 per cent per year between 1989 and 1994. The labour force continued to expand by about 4 per cent (400 000 new entrants) a year. The civil service (including parastatals) expanded fast throughout the 1980s, increasing its employment by an average of over 5 per cent each year; but real wages eroded substantially. The average real wage (private and public) in 1993 stood at only 45 per cent of its 1985 level. Although participation in the urban informal sector also grew fast in the early 1990s (14 per cent annually), by 1993 the estimated urban unemployment rate exceeded 20 per cent (World Bank, 1993b).

In Uganda, political and economic instability from 1978 to 1981 resulted in further declines in GDP, consumption and taxation revenues, alongside rising inflation. The economic problems reinforced the view of the Military Commission and the Tanzanians that re-establishment of Obote was desirable. The first years of Obote II did see some economic recovery. Under a stabilisation programme supported by the IMF and the World Bank, economic growth revived to over 4 per cent annually, with positive movements in per capita consumption, per capita food production, the real wage, the investment rate and the revenue ratio. Yet the escalating military conflict, especially from 1984 with the devastating killings in the Luwero Triangle, brought economic recovery to a halt.

From 1986, when Museveni acquired power, the economy recovered significantly, with the support of IMF and World Bank programmes and finance. Per capita incomes rose; the contraction of social programmes reversed; educational enrolment rates, water coverage and doctor availability improved (Table 4.3). Economic growth averaged 6 per cent annually from 1986 to 1995, but it did not translate proportionately into rising private consumption; some went to restore government revenues and some to rising investment. Consumption per capita rose annually by a modest 1.5 per cent, with small improvements in calorie availability and food production. High inflation came under control, falling from 250 per cent to 6 per cent annually between 1987 and 1995. Tax revenue recovered, permitting a rise in social expenditure, although defence maintained and even increased its share over the period as a whole. Enrolment rates rose from 57 per cent in 1984 to 71 per cent in 1992 (primary) and from 8 per cent to 13 per cent (secondary). Health facilities were rehabilitated and immunisation rates climbed from below 10 per cent in 1986 to over 60 per cent in 1990.

Despite improved economic performance in Uganda since 1986 and continuing pressures in Kenya, it remains clear that Kenya has had far superior overall outcomes since independence — not only in higher aggregate economic growth, except after 1990, but also because the government maintained its revenue at a much higher proportion of GDP, especially in the catastrophic period towards the end of Amin's rule. It also secured a much higher proportion of government expenditure for social services because of the substantially lower proportion of expenditure on defence (Table 4.2). Consequently, Kenya has had persistently better social indicators, the only exception being per capita food availability at the beginning and end of the period. Infant mortality rates in Kenya, 84 per cent of Uganda's in 1960, reached just 54 per cent of the Ugandan level by 1990.

At first glance, it might appear that the comparative aggregate economic and social performances of Kenya and Uganda support the view that poor economic and social performance leads to instability and conflict. Yet closer inspection of the *timing* of the conflict in Uganda relative to the behaviour of the economy suggests that this conclusion is too simple and largely incorrect. The first source of post-independence instability in Uganda — the overthrow of Obote by Amin — followed a period of relatively good economic and social performance, not markedly different from that of Kenya where no such instability occurred. Amin himself then undermined the economy and the government's ability to meet social needs, with dire results.

The economic collapse during the Amin regime contributed to its demise in 1979, in several senses. Economic and social as well as political chaos inspired the 1978-79 invasion by UNLF — doubtless there would have been less enthusiasm for the revolt had social and economic performance been going well. People whom the Amin regime had harmed economically through the generalised economic disintegration welcomed and joined the invading forces — including the peasants as well as those he had attacked directly, notably the middle classes and especially the intellectuals. Moreover, the collapse of government revenue had made it difficult for him to sustain the armed forces. Despite a virtual tripling of the budget share going to defence (from 7.5 per cent on average in Obote I to 22.4 per cent), revenue declines, especially towards the end of the period, led to a fall in real expenditures and in the share of GDP going to defence (to 1.3 per cent from 5 per cent between 1972 and 1979). This episode can be seen, perhaps, as endorsing the view that weak economic performance can give rise to violence. The confusion and corruption endemic in the immediate post-Amin era helped lead to the successive replacement of presidents until Obote was restored, also lending some support to this view.

The next major instability arose as the NRA gained adherents and Obote's forces reacted with enormous ferocity from 1984 to 1985. This episode *followed* a period of recovery of the economy when many indicators had just started to move in a positive direction, thus apparently refuting the hypothesis that weak economic performance causes violence. The killings arose to some extent, however, because Obote's soldiers had gone out of control, owing partly to their very low pay, a consequence of the weak revenue capacity of the government. Moreover, popular support from 1980 for the National Resistance Movement and Army of Museveni undoubtedly arose partially from the economic impoverishment of the Amin and post-Amin years. According to Okoth, "Untold sufferings of the masses ... gave rise to popular insurrection" (Okoth, 1996, p. 56). Conversely, the years after 1986 generally brought economic recovery and improved social performance — yet conflicts remained endemic in some areas. Again, it appears that improving aggregate performance does not prevent the persistence of violent conflict.

The clearest conclusion arising from comparisons of the behaviour of the Kenyan and Ugandan economies is that violence and instability *worsen* economic and social performance. At times, poor economic performance and government revenue shortages appear to have fuelled resistance; but in general the comparison does not provide strong support for the view that aggregate economic impoverishment *causes* instability and violence[1]. Conversely, however, the relatively better outcomes in Kenya seem to have served to create vested interests in the stability of the system. (Nor can one argue from this evidence that Fund/Bank programmes caused conflict; for Uganda they tended to be associated with economic recovery.) It is perhaps not surprising that aggregate economic performance does not appear to explain violence, since it is the *relative* entitlements and the perceived costs of conflict to different groups which are likely to motivate conflict, as suggested in the framework described above.

Inequities and Imbalances

Both Kenya and Uganda show evidence of inequalities in economic and social entitlements. Because the colonial authorities drew local administrative boundaries along ethnic lines, regional imbalances in the distribution of entitlements imply corresponding ones among ethnic groups, which may make them politically explosive. Both countries inherited significant imbalances at independence, stemming partly from differences in climate and fertility and partly from policy. In Uganda, the colonial regime favoured the southern part of the country[2] and thus accentuated inequalities already in evidence in pre-colonial times. In each country, the capital stood in the highly fertile areas and the region surrounding it (called the Central region/province) was privileged in infrastructure and economic opportunities during colonialism relative to the rest of the country and especially the north. The Northern region in Uganda and the Northeast province in Kenya suffered social and economic deprivation. One simple measure of the extent of disparities — the coefficient of variation in average household income across provinces/regions — shows a remarkable similarity between the two countries in the late 1960s, with Kenya exhibiting the higher variation even when Nairobi is excluded (Table 4.12). The data on inequalities reviewed below are not strictly comparable between the two countries, in dates or dimensions, for any category. Moreover, because Kenya has seven provinces and Uganda only four regions, greater disparities might be expected in Kenya.

Social Infrastructure

Uganda had a fairly even distribution of water availability (measured by boreholes per person) in 1961, with the Northern and Western regions worst off (Table 4.4). The disparities appear to have increased by the 1990s while the ranking had reversed, with Northern region on top and Central region at the bottom. Data for safe water coverage in the 1990s show the Central and Northern populations best at 28 per cent, but with only small disparities from the Eastern (25 per cent) and Western (22 per cent) regions. Disparities in Kenya in 1974/75 (excluding Northeast for which data are lacking) resembled those in Uganda, with Western and Central provinces best-placed in terms of population within one mile of a water source in the dry season, almost twice as well off as the worst, Coast (Table 4.4). Over time, the disparities increased significantly in Uganda. Although no comparable evidence over time exists for Kenya, survey data collected in 1993, which differentiates among the main ethnic groups, suggests that access to water in the home was highest for Kikuyu (albeit at only one in three), and lowest for Kalenjin (fewer than one in ten) (Kenya National Council for Population and Development *et al.*, 1993).

Table 4.4. **Regional Distribution of Water Availability in Kenya and Uganda**

	Kenya			Uganda		
Province	Households within One Mile of Water in Dry Season 1974/75		Region	Population per Borehole (Ratio)[a]		Per Cent of Population with Safe Water
	Per Cent	Ratio[a]		1961	1990s	1990s
Central	83	1.9	Central	1.60	1.0	28
Coast	43	1.0	Western	1.00	1.2	22
Eastern	61	1.4	Eastern	1.50	1.5	25
Nyanza	70	1.6	Northern	1.00	2.7	28
Western	80	1.9				
Rift Valley	70	1.6				
Northeast	N/A	N/A				
National	72					
Coefficient of Variation	0.29			0.266	0.476	0.112

Note: a) The ratios are index numbers, with the lowest value (least well-off province or region) set equal to 1.0 and the other values calculated in relation to it.

Sources: Republic of Uganda (1966a,b); World Bank (1993a); UNDP (1996); Republic of Kenya (1981).

In social infrastructure, Uganda's Western region remained least endowed by most measures of health facilities from 1970 to the 1990s, with the Central region, including Kampala, among the best (Table 4.5). The Northern region, as poorly off as the Western in 1970, gained in hospital beds per person by 1991, while other regions and the nation as a whole fell back. The Northern region remained the laggard in distance from a primary health care centre.

Kenya made better overall progress in its health sector. It introduced free medical treatment in government facilities in 1965 and the network expanded significantly after the central government assumed responsibility for rural health services in 1970. Widening access to health care during the 1960s and 1970s, together with rising incomes and better education, brought significant improvements in the nation's aggregate health status[3]. Kenya had regional disparities in health services in 1974/75 similar to those of Uganda, but Nyanza province was much the worst-placed in access to nearby health care (Table 4.5). There remain quite marked ethnic differences in the availability of government-provided care. Survey data on health care provided by ethnicity suggest that Kalenjin rely most heavily on public care — 62 per cent, compared to a national average of less than 29 per cent — while the Kikuyu and the Luyha tend to use facilities provided by religious organisations (Kenya National Council for Population and Development *et al.*, 1993).

41

Table 4.5. **Regional Distribution of Health Facilities in Kenya and Uganda**

Kenya			Uganda			
Province	Households within Eight Miles of a Health Care Centre, 1974/75		Region	Hospital Beds per Person (Ratio)[a]		Km. to a Primary Care Centre
	Per Cent	Ratio[a]		1970	1991	1992/93
Central	91	9	Central	2.1	1.8	9.3
Coast	66	6.5	Western	1.0	1.0	7.7
Eastern	69	6.8	Eastern	1.6	1.0	7.4
Nyanza	10	1.0	Northern	1.0	1.8	11.3
Western	80	5.3				
Rift Valley	54	7.9				
Northeast	N/A	N/A				
National	78					
Coefficient of Variation	0.459			0.373	0.33	0.201

Note: a) The ratio is an index with the lowest value (worst-off province or region) set equal to one and other values calculated against it.

Sources: Republic of Uganda (1972), World Bank (1993a), Republic of Uganda (1996b).

In education, Uganda showed no big regional differences in primary or secondary enrolment; the Western region fared worst in both 1968 and 1990 in primary education, while the previously privileged position of Central region disappeared by 1990 (Table 4.6). Northern region made the most substantial improvements in primary education, achieving an enrolment rate of 85 per cent (the highest of the regions) in 1990. Secondary enrolment in the Eastern and Northern regions was significantly lower than in the Central and Western ones in 1990. Disparities were much greater in Kenya than in Uganda in both primary and secondary education for each date for which evidence is available; but much of this arises from the very weak position of the Northeast, with enrolment rates of only 13 per cent (primary) in 1980 and 1 per cent (secondary) in 1974/75. Kenya had a much higher aggregate level of achievement, however. Education was accorded central importance as a route to social and economic mobility. Its perceived value is reflected in its importance in *harambee* efforts (voluntary fund-raising), and its priority in expenditures even among households living below the poverty line (UNICEF/ODA/AMREF, 1995, p. 18).

Aggregate changes in primary enrolment show surges following the abolition of fees for grades I-IV in 1974 in Kenya, with uneven access across provinces and income groups. In the mid-1970s, recurrent public expenditures on education, per capita, ranged from almost five pounds in Central province to less than one in Northeastern. Nonetheless, provincial trends to the mid-1970s suggest considerable equalisation in primary enrolment (Bigsten, 1977), with the largest increases in provinces that had the lowest bases, including Nyanza, Rift Valley and Western, with increases of 192, 170 and 154 per cent respectively, compared to 37 and 50 per cent increases in Nairobi and Central province.

Table 4.6. **Regional Distribution of Education in Kenya and Uganda**
(Enrolment Rates in Per Cent)

	Kenya				Uganda		
Province	Primary		Secondary (net)	Region	Primary		Secondary (net)
	1975	1980	1974/75		1968	1990	1990
Central	105	102	18	Central	38	69	11
Coast	61	68	11	Western	31	68	12
Eastern	101	108	7	Eastern	35	79	8
Nyanza	93	97	7	Northern	37	85	9
Western	70	93	6				
Rift Valley	105	119	8				
Northeast	8	13	1				
Coefficient of Variation	0.455	0.417	0.63		0.087	0.109	0.183

Sources: Republic of Uganda (1973); World Bank (1993a); Republic of Kenya (1981); Bigsten (1977); Heyer (1990).

Primary enrolment by district still showed pockets of very low enrolment in the late 1980s. In 1987, 12 of the 41 districts had primary enrolment rates below 70 per cent, particularly in the arid and semi-arid lands but also in Nairobi and Mombasa which, at 63 per cent and 64 per cent respectively, fell far below many rural areas. Rates of enrolment in the arid areas are reportedly as low as 2 per cent among pastoral children, for example in Turkana (Barrow, 1995). Moreover, differing shares of qualified teachers, which ranged in 1976 from 98 per cent and 82 per cent in Nairobi and Central province to 50 per cent or 60 per cent for other provinces, suggest significant differences in quality of education. Survey data indicate that literacy levels in the 1990s still remained significantly higher among the Kikuyu, among whom 72 per cent could "read easily" compared to less than half of the Kalenjin and about 63 per cent of the Luo and Luyha (Kenya National Council for Population and Development *et al.,* 1993).

In general, both countries had regional disparities in physical infrastructure, with some tendency towards greater divergence from more generous average levels in Kenya. In both nations, the Central region (province) tended to do best, partly because it contained the capital, while the North in Uganda and the Northeast in Kenya lagged. The privileged position of Uganda's Central region significantly lessened by the 1990s, however, with definite improvement in the North. Differentials in Kenya also apparently narrowed but, unfortunately, little evidence exists to show changes over time.

Economic Opportunities

Wage employment forms a critical dimension of potential entitlements in Kenya and Uganda, as elsewhere. Recent analysis of Kenyan household microdata has confirmed that the best-off rural households make up the small minority whose heads work in the formal public and private sectors (World Bank, 1995a, p. 21), despite a significant decline in formal sector wages over the last decade. The extent of wage employment also provides an indicator of economic integration.

At independence, Uganda had wage employment fairly equally distributed among the population; the Central, Eastern and Northern regions each accounted for about a fifth of the total, but with a disproportionate concentration of both public and private jobs in the Western region. From 1962 to 1970, the Central and Eastern regions benefited most from the rapid expansion in employment, while the Northern region lagged, being particularly weak in the public sector where employment grew at only half the national rate; thus the increase of paid employment during the first Obote regime showed no bias towards the North despite Obote's own origins. This may reflect the near inevitability of growth concentration closer to the capital.

Evidence for the late 1980s and early 1990s suggests a much greater concentration of employment in the Central region, with the Eastern and especially the Northern regions lagging. For example, in 1991, the proportion of wage employment in the Central region reached more than one and a half times its share in population, while the Northern figure was only just over half of its population share (Table 4.7). The disparity is greater in high-quality jobs. The Central region had 54 per cent and 59 per cent of male manager and male professional jobs respectively, with only 29 per cent of the population; the Northern region, with 19 per cent of the population, claimed only 11 per cent and 10 per cent of such jobs[4].

Table 4.7. **Formal Employment Opportunities by Region, Kenya and Uganda**

	Kenya				Uganda			
Province	Per Cent of Work Force in Employment, 1994			Region	Ratio of Share of Employment to Share of Population			
					Total			Firms[a]
	Public	Private	Total		1962	1970	1991	1989
Central	3.6	12.0	15.6	Central	0.81	0.84	1.62	2.6
Eastern	2.3	5.8	8.1	Western	1.55	1.19	0.91	0.34
Nyanza	1.9	4.5	6.4	Eastern	0.84	0.98	0.71	0.50
Western	2.1	4.0	6.1	Northern	0.9	0.96	0.56	0.16
Rift Valley	2.5	5.9	8.4					
Northeast	2.4	2.1	4.5					
Nairobi	6.1	19.6	25.7					
Coefficient of Variation:								
Excl. Nairobi	0.241	0.591	0.476		0.343	0.147	0.493	1.269
Total	0.495	0.790	0.704					

Note: a) Enterprises with five or more employees.
Sources: Republic of Kenya, *Statistical Abstracts*, various editions; Republic of Uganda (1996b).

Surveys indicate that the formal business sector and small-scale, non-agricultural activities have also concentrated disproportionately in the Central and, to a lesser extent, the Western regions. The Northern region has had many fewer of these activities, especially the formal business sector, and a larger proportion of household agricultural activities, typically associated with lower incomes; for Uganda as a whole, value added per employee in business enterprises amounted to sh 584 000 (1989) as against sh 124 000 (1992-93) in small-scale and household enterprises (price adjustments between these years would increase the difference).

In Kenya, the Central province also had the highest proportion of the population in both public and private employment in 1994 (Table 4.7). The Northeast fared the worst. Households engaged in "subsistence farming", which World Bank analysis associates with the highest incidence of poverty (46 per cent in 1992), prevailed in Nyanza and Eastern provinces. Pastoral activity, also with high poverty incidence (42 per cent), is most common in Northeastern province. Kenya has more marked provincial differences in access to private sector employment. Except for Nairobi, public sector jobs seem fairly equally distributed across the provinces, ranging from 2 per cent to 3.6 per cent of the population. The coefficient of variation shows falling disparities in Uganda in the 1960s, and then a sharp widening to 1991, with the disparities similar in Kenya and Uganda in the 1990s.

Both countries have allocated civil service jobs on a tribal basis. Bienen (1974) noted this for Kenya in 1969, when Kikuyu held 29 per cent of the upper-level jobs, with Luyha and Luo relatively over-represented as well. In the 1980s, affirmative action programmes increased minority tribe participation, in practice benefiting the Kalenjin. At the senior levels, Kalenjin representation has increased significantly. Similarly, in Uganda government jobs have tended to go predominantly to the President's tribe. Although Museveni made an initial effort to bring in people from all over the country, observers today point to the disproportionate employment of Ankole in the capital.

Incomes and Poverty

Directly comparable per capita income data are lacking, but making the most of what is available (Table 4.8) shows differentials among provinces/regions markedly higher in Kenya than in Uganda in the early period. In Kenya, they widened until 1975 — when average household income in Coast province was estimated at seven times that of the worst-off province (the Northeast) — but they narrowed considerably from 1975 to 1994, when the ratio (excluding Nairobi) had dropped to 1.9[5]. In Uganda, differentials seem also to have narrowed somewhat over the years. For 1970, Jamal (1991) estimated that the South, with 35 per cent to 40 per cent of the population, had 75 per cent to 80 per cent of the national income. Estimates for 1992 show the Central region, with 28 per cent of the population, taking 44 per cent of the income, while the Central and Western regions together accounted for 56 per cent of the population and 67 per cent of national income. The coefficient of variation also fell.

Table 4.8. **Regional Income Disparities in Kenya and Uganda**

	Kenya				Uganda	
Province	Ratio of Per Capita Income to that of the Poorest Province			Region	Share of Higher Rural Taxpayers[a]	Expenditure Per Capita[a]
	1967	1975	1994		1969	1992
Central	2.6	4.3	1.1	Central	2.9	2.1[b]
Coast[c]	4.5	7.1	1.9	Western	1.7	1.7
Eastern	1.6	2.6	1.0	Eastern/Northern	1.0	1.0
Nyanza	1.8	2.5	1.2			
Western	1.1	1.8	1.2			
Rift Valley	2.6	4.0	1.5			
Northeast	1.0	1.0	1.5			
Nairobi	21.7	31.3	3.7			
Coefficient of Variation:						
Excl. Nairobi	0.557	0.608	0.231		0.501	0.412
Incl. Nairobi	1.516	1.475	0.538			

Notes: *a)* Ratio of value for the region to that for the poorest region; *b)* includes Kampala; *c)* includes Mombasa.
Sources: UNDP (1996); Republic of Uganda (1972); Bigsten (1977); Republic of Kenya (1996).

The rank ordering of income among regions in Uganda remained the same, with the Central region followed by the Western best-off and the Eastern/Northern regions worst-off. In Kenya, as in Uganda, the central and southern parts of the country did best in the early period and the Northeast worst until 1975. Then, while Nairobi and the Coast (which includes the second largest city, Mombasa) remained on top, Central and Rift Valley provinces saw some deterioration and the Northeast gained. The provincial distribution of income in Kenya thus has changed markedly since independence, with a significant closing of inherited gaps. The nation's capital has enjoyed an enormous income advantage over the rest of the country, with average incomes practically ten times those of all other provinces except Coast (the clear second runner) in 1967, but falling considerably in relative terms since 1975[6]. Rift Valley and Northeast provinces became tied by 1994 for third place, formerly occupied by Central province which fell to seventh[7]. This accords with the statement reported by a Kitui (Central province) resident that "...Ten years ago we were rich — you could see it in the local markets that were functioning. Today there is nothing to sell. There are no markets any more" (UNICEF/ODA/AMREF, 1995, p. vii).

Poverty rates in Kenya, as indicated by the proportion of households in the bottom quintile of the expenditure distribution, appeared lowest in Central and Northeast provinces in 1981-82, and twice as high or more in Eastern, Nyanza and Western provinces (Table 4.9). Evidence on aggregate trends in poverty since Kenyan independence suggests that the picture improved through the mid-1970s, deteriorated somewhat to 1982, then worsened significantly, at least to 1992. District data indicate considerable variations among districts within each province, confirming the presence of economic heterogeneity within ethno-regional groups. In Uganda, the Central and Western regions had the lowest rural poverty rates and Eastern and Northern regions the highest in both 1969 and 1990-91. The variation in poverty rates across regions remained higher in Uganda throughout, especially in the early 1990s. Rural poverty rates were high everywhere in Uganda in 1990-91, over 50 per cent in Central region and over 90 per cent in Northern region.

Table 4.9. **Poverty Rates in Kenya and Uganda**

Kenya			Uganda		
Province	Per Cent in Bottom Quintile		Region	Per Cent of Taxpayers with Incomes below sh 1 000	Per Cent of Population below Poverty Line
	1981-82	1994		1969	1989
Central	11	34.2	Central	50	51
Coast	16	32.9	Western	85	61
Eastern	26	47.5	Eastern	91	68
Nyanza	22	42.1	Northern	80	44
Western	23	48.6	Major Towns	16	Note[a]
Rift Valley	17	37.2			
Northeast	11	28.4			
Nairobi	8	18.9			
Coefficient of Variation:					
Excl. Nairobi	0.163	0.197	Excluding Major Towns	0.238	0.384[b]
Incl. Nairobi	0.388	0.275	Including Towns	0.486	0.486

Notes: a) Major towns are included in the regional figures; b) based on data for 1990-91.
Sources: Republic of Uganda (1972); Republic of Kenya (1996); World Bank (1993b).

Social Well-Being

In Uganda, social indicators reveal a pattern of regional disparities similar to those in income: the Central region was ranked at the top for adult literacy, infant and child mortality rates (IMR) and life expectancy, with the Northern region almost always at the bottom (Table 4.10). These differences, which were already apparent in the 1960s, remained into the 1990s for the one indicator — infant mortality rates — available throughout on a regional basis. The gap widened in the 1960s as the IMR fell faster in the Central region than in the North but narrowed slightly between 1969 and 1991, when it was a third higher in the North than in the Central region. For most indicators, the Western region ranks second and the Eastern region third. Current human resources reflect past imbalances in educational opportunities: for example, despite improving enrolments, the Northern region continues to lag behind the rest of the country in adult literacy.

Table 4.10. **Trends in Social Indicators: Kenya and Uganda**

Province	Kenya IMR[a] per 1 000 live births	Adult Literacy %	Children Stunted[b]		Region	Uganda IMR[a] per 1 000 live births			Adult Literacy %
	1979	1982	1977	1994		1959	1969	1991	1991
Central	85	65	31	29	Central	150	99	105	67
Coast	206	45	19	38	Western	163	121	125	51
Eastern	129	48	38	39	Eastern	178	139	122	50
Nyanza	220	39	25	36	Northern	170	142	141	43
Rift Valley	132	41	29	32	National	165	125	123	54
Western	187	48	21	37					
Northeast	160	N/A	N/A	26					
Coeff. of Variation	0.30	0.19	0.26	0.15		0.07	0.16	0.12	0.19

Notes: a) IMR is the infant mortality rate; b) percentage of children aged 1-5 whose height is two standard deviations below the norm.

Sources: Republic of Kenya (1996); Kaplinsky (1978); Heyer (1990); Republic of Uganda, *1960 Population Census*, Vol. IV; World Bank (1993a); Republic of Uganda (1996b).

The UNDP's Human Development Index (HDI) includes both social and economic indicators. For Uganda (Table 4.11), it shows the Northern region 20 per cent below the national average in 1992 — eleven ranks below Uganda's world ranking (eighth from the worst). Central region lay 20 per cent above the national average (15 ranks above Uganda's world ranking). Eastern and Western regions came fairly close to the national average.

Table 4.11. **Uganda: Human Development Index by Region, 1991**

	Central	Eastern	Northern	Western
Adjusted Real GDP per Capita	155.5	82.6	75.1	83.0
Adult Literacy	67.2	49.9	43.2	51.0
Educational Attainment Index[a]	111.8	94.6	84.9	95.9
Life Expectancy	49	49	43.6	48.9
HDI, 1992[a]	119.2	97.9	80.8	95.9

Note: a) Uganda national average = 100.
Source: UNDP (1996).

While Kenya's regional gaps exceeded those for Uganda's social indicators, the lack of a persistent pattern may make them less explosive politically. Kenya had disparities in infant mortality greater than Uganda's in 1979, mainly because of the relatively low rate in Central province (including Nairobi), while its adult literacy disparities in 1982 resembled Uganda's in 1991 (Tables 4.10 and 4.12). Nyanza ranked worst on both measures. The only indicator available over time by province is child malnutrition, a sensitive indicator of social well-being; stunting indicates past, and wasting current, malnutrition. Stunting shows (Table 4.10) an overall worsening since the late 1970s, with no consistent pattern across provinces.

Conclusions on Regional Disparities

Both countries showed significant regional disparities in both input and output indicators (Table 4.12). The available data suggest Uganda's regional disparities were smaller than Kenya's in social services and infant mortality rates, similar for literacy and malnutrition, and greater (in the 1990s) in incomes and poverty rates. Kenya has narrowed some of its gaps since the mid-1970s. In Uganda, the deprived North has improved in infrastructure and seen some closing of the income gaps, but disparities in average incomes remain high with increasing regional variation in employment and poverty.

Table 4.12. **Regional Disparities as Measured by Coefficients of Variation in Selected Economic and Social Indicators**

	Kenya		Uganda	
	Period	Coefficient	Period	Coefficient
Education Services				
Primary	1975	0.455	1968	0.087
	1980	0.417	1990	0.109
Secondary	1975	0.630	1990	0.183
Health Services				
Distance to Centres	1974/75	0.458	1992/93	0.201
Hospital Beds per Person			1970	0.373
			1991	0.330
Water				
Distance to Water	1974/75	0.290		
Boreholes per Person			1961	0.266
			1990s	0.476
Safe Water Coverage			1990s	0.112
Employment			1962	0.343
			1970	0.147
Excluding Nairobi	1994	0.476	1991	0.493
Including Nairobi	1994	0.704		
Incomes per Household	1967	0.567[a]	1969	0.501
	1975	0.608[a]		
	1994	0.231[a]	1992	0.412
Poverty			1969[b]	0.238
			1969[c]	0.486
	1994	0.163	1990/91[b]	0.348
			1990/91[c]	0.486
Infant Mortality Rates			1959	0.073
	1979	0.300	1969	0.157
			1991	0.122
Adult Literacy	1982	0.194	1991	0.192
Malnutrition	1977	0.258		
	1994	0.163	1990s	0.126

Notes: a) Excluding Nairobi; b) excluding towns; c) including towns.
Sources: Tables 4.4 to 4.10.

49

Gaps in economic opportunities, incomes and social indicators persist in each country. The central regions/provinces containing the capital were at independence and in most respects remained the most privileged areas. In Kenya, Central province ranked among the top two provinces on ten indicators and never among the bottom two. In Uganda, Central region had the best indicator in 12 cases and the worst in three. In both countries, one region/province did markedly worse than the others — Northern region in Uganda (the worst on eight indicators and the best on three) and the Northeast in Kenya (among the worst two in seven cases and the best in just one). Uganda's Eastern region came second in deprivation. The Northern region showed definite signs of improvement by the 1990s in access to health, water and education services, but this did not occur in Kenya's Northeast. Nyanza and Coast provinces also showed fairly persistent signs of deprivation.

This evidence alone would not suggest that uneven development can explain the violence in Uganda compared with Kenya, but interaction with political factors undoubtedly gave it a role. In both countries, the most deprived area has generated violence — the Shifta wars in Kenya's Northeast and violent rebellion from Uganda's North when leaders from that region are not in power. In Kenya, the Northeast is a relatively marginalised place which can be neglected with a certain impunity; it contains only 2 per cent of the population. Nyanza, home of the Luo and accounting for 17 per cent of the population (very similar to the 19 per cent in the Northern region in Uganda), could potentially offer much more serious opposition. It performed among the worst in infant mortality rates, health facilities and adult literacy in the mid to late 1970s and its per capita income was just 60 per cent of that of Central province (excluding Nairobi). Moreover, the Luo were denied significant political participation and their leader, Oginga Odinga, was imprisoned under Kenyatta and his political party outlawed. Nonetheless, a culture of violent opposition did not emerge, for several possible reasons. From the mid-1960s to the mid-1970s, Kenya enjoyed general economic and social advance with per capita income growth at 2.7 per cent per year on average. Nyanza shared in this, with per capita income rising only slightly less than the national average. It also experienced progress in health, education and water services. From the mid-1970s, when per capita income growth slowed, differentials narrowed sharply so that in 1994 Nyanza had slightly higher per capita income than Central province. Its poverty rate was high, with 42 per cent of the population in the bottom 40 per cent of household expenditure. Selected districts in Nyanza showed poverty rates of 46 per cent and 56 per cent. The malnutrition rate (stunting) was 43 per cent in 1994, substantially above the 1977 level. Yet these high rates were not the worst in the country and seem low compared with the rate of over 90 per cent in the Northern region of Uganda in both 1969 and 1990-91. Thus the absolute performance was much better than in the comparable deprived areas of Uganda.

In Uganda, inherited political and military institutions gave the deprivations political significance. While colonial and agroclimatic factors favoured the development of the Central and Western regions and disadvantaged the North, Northerners dominated the army — a key factor in Northern preponderance in government until 1986 when defeat of the UNLF by Museveni forces eliminated Northern primacy in the army.

Moreover, much of the post-independence history of conflict reflected attempts by the Buganda (in the Centre) to protect their economic privileges against attack by the Northern-controlled regimes of Obote and Amin — Buganda resistance to incorporation into the Ugandan Republic, still a source of potential tension, for example. Conversely, Obote's attack on the Buganda in 1966 and again, much more viciously, in the 1980s, can be seen as a reflection of Northern resentment against these perceived advantages. Amin's violence was more random and less co-ordinated, but he too attacked economic privilege and especially the Buganda, with the aim of redistributing resources to his own people.

The persistent Northern insurrection during the Museveni regime undoubtedly has stemmed from the economic and social deprivation of the region; small amounts of money offered by rebel leaders attract youths to take up arms; and both extreme poverty and low levels of literacy may make people more open to conversion to the Holy Spirit Movement. Data for Gulu, Arua and Kitgum, three areas badly affected by the fighting, shows they all have had very poor development indicators, but not systematically worse than the Northern region as a whole (Table 4.13)

Table 4.13. **Deprivation in Uganda's Northern War Districts**

	Arua	Gulu	Kitgum	Northern Region	Uganda
Infant Mortality Rates, 1990	137	172	165	141	122
Literacy Rates, 1990	46	49	39	43	54
Access to Water, 1989	23	54	29	42	31
Primary Enrolment, 1989	69	53	102	72	72
Secondary Enrolment, 1989	11	8	6	8	14
Population per Government Health Unit, 1991, thousands	17.3	21.1	17.6	16.2	19.5
Population per Doctor, 1991, thousands	52.1	42.3	38.9	57.9	27.1
Income Share of the Bottom Quartile of the Population	33	38	64	43	25

Sources: UNDP (1996); World Bank (1996*b*); Bigsten (1995).

In Kenya, the relative advantages of the Kikuyu continue to be resented. To some extent the non-Kikuyu (Moi) regime has acted to mollify these resentments with civil service recruitment and the distribution of state patronage. More important, however, and in contrast to Uganda's first 25 years of independence, both Kikuyu and non-Kikuyu regimes succeeded in expanding economic opportunities and providing services in ways that extended interests in favour of political stability. The common belief among Kenyans that the system did provide opportunities for them and their children is reflected in significant private expenditures on education, a clear investment in the future. Kenya's strategy succeeded in that the disparities in opportunities inherited at independence lessened over time, allowing the fruits to flow to the wider population. It put Kenya in relatively good stead even when, from the mid-1980s, aggregate economic growth slowed and the incidence of poverty worsened.

Access to Land

In agrarian societies, competition for land can constitute a source of conflict. This has been argued as important in Rwanda, for example. Uganda has over four times more land per person than Rwanda but less than half that of Kenya (Table 4.14), suggesting a possible reason for the greater violence in Uganda. Yet Bangladesh, for example, has a population density considerably greater even than Rwanda's, so population density and conflict clearly do not have a mechanical relationship.

Table 4.14. **Hectares per Rural Person, Selected Countries**

Bangladesh	0.2
Rwanda	0.4
Uganda	1.5
Kenya	3.1
Tanzania	4.4

Sources: UNDP (1996); World Bank, *World Development Report 1995.*

In neither Uganda nor Kenya was land a primary source of violent conflict; in fact, despite Kenya's more favourable person/land ratio, the land question has had more political importance there than in Uganda. Observers have noted that it figures far more centrally in the language of political conflict than in most African states (Weeks and Young, 1996), yet has not resulted in violent conflict for much of the period. Although Uganda has greater pressure on land, landless farm labourers have a much higher prevalence in Kenya, accounting for 9 per cent of the male workforce compared with less than 3 per cent in Uganda (Berg-Schlosser and Siegler, 1990). Most observers see little evidence of land scarcity in much of Uganda, among them Gashumba, Director of the Agricultural Secretariat. He has estimated that less than a third of the cultivable land in Uganda is in use. According to Kigula[8], recent research has shown that all have access to land if they want it, *via* borrowing, inheritance and so on. Nsibambi concluded in a review of the land issue in Uganda: "Uganda does have enough fertile land and ... landlessness has not yet become a critical issue in Uganda" [in Rupesinghe (ed.), 1989, p. 224].

In general, all Uganda's regions have adequate potential for providing for their own subsistence and growing food and non-food cash crops, although the Northern region is the worst-endowed in terms of quality of land and its use, and the Central and Western regions are the most fertile. The Central and Eastern regions have the highest ratios of people to land, while the Northern region has a ratio less than half that of Central region. Data for the early 1990s show that the Eastern and Central regions have the highest proportions of land devoted to farmland (excluding lakes), with the Central region having the most large farms. The Northern region has the smallest proportions of farmland, large-scale farms and coffee plantings.

The growing pressure of population on land in Uganda, together with the *Mailo* system of land tenure and other forms of private property, has nonetheless led to the marginalisation of peasants in some areas, where they have been forced onto smaller and more infertile plots. For example, in Teso (Eastern region) land per capita fell by more than half from 1948 to 1982, while in Acholi it dropped more sharply. In the more densely populated areas, holdings have fragmented as a result. A 1982 survey of four districts in different parts of the country found that over half the peasants in each farmed plots of less than two hectares. It estimated that despite significant fractions of household land not under cultivation in all areas other than Teso, around 90 per cent of families had inadequate land[9].

There is evidence of growing land shortage in some areas of Uganda, especially in the Southwest. Open land has disappeared in Bushenyi and Mbarara in Western region as population pressure has increased (Kasfir, 1988). In some areas, land pressure has caused land disputes, which can become violent. A Cabinet Committee reporting on disputes in Kasese district in the Western region between the Bakonjo cultivators and Basongora cattle keepers found that "the land disputes in Kasese district are not ethnically motivated but essentially a result of shortage of land. The Basongora and Bakonjo have undoubtedly lived with each other at different times ... and the current land disputes have just assumed ethnic overtones which have blown out of proportion" (Republic of Uganda, 1996c, p. 25). The Committee feared that the dispute might degenerate into hostilities without action to alleviate the situation.

Most land disputes in Uganda occur among people of the same ethnicity, often within the same family. A comparison of disputes in a few districts found that the major cause in a high dispute area, Kabala, was high population pressure aggravated by widespread polygamy, the return of voluntary migrants and the weakness of the non-farm economy. In other districts such as Masaka and Kabarole, monogamy, out-migration and off-farm opportunities reduced population pressure. Forms of land tenure can also cause dispute, especially where richer farmers try to evict customary tenants. Land disputes are rare in the less densely populated Northern region (Kigula, 1993, 1996).

Even if Kenya has less adverse overall population/land ratios, rapid population growth has been associated with a dramatic fall in the average size of rural landholdings since independence, with some regional variation (Table 4.15). The share of households with less than two acres rose from less than 18 per cent to over 25 per cent in the decade to 1992. Most poor households have very small parcels of land. The pressure on holdings is most marked in Central province with over 83 per cent below one hectare and pockets of very high poverty incidence. Rift Valley also has about 57 per cent of holdings below one hectare, as does a majority in Western province.

Table 4.15. **Trends in Landholding in Kenya, 1982-1992, by Province**

Province	Average Size of Holding (Acres)		Per Cent of Households with Less than Two Acres	
	1982	1992	1982	1992
Coast	5.2	3.8	10.3	9.8
Eastern	6.9	5.4	8.9	22.3
Central	3.0	2.2	41.0	41.5
Rift Valley	4.9	4.7	15.4	20.1
Nyanza	4.9	3.5	7.1	19.1
Western	4.7	4.1	20.2	30.9
National Average	4.9	4.0	17.7	25.1

Source: World Bank (1995a), Table 1.6.

Kenya is one of the few African countries that undertook widespread land adjudication and title programmes. The British promoted reform of tenure from a communal system to an individual (freehold) basis in Central province following the Swynnerton Plan in 1954; reform accelerated and expanded after independence. By 1983 when the pace slowed, about 10 per cent of the total land area was registered. In the high-potential Central, Nyanza and Western provinces almost three-quarters of registrable land had been registered, whereas the Coast and Northeastern provinces still have seen little adjudication and titling. Two outcomes of this process relate to potential conflict. First, the distribution of landholdings has remained skewed, particularly in the medium- and high-potential regions. Only about one-third of the former settler estates were officially subdivided, so that local elites obtained transfers of large holdings intact. The large farms, generally located in well-endowed areas, average 1 000 hectares, compared to a mean small-farm size of less than two hectares.

Second, post-independence policies have significantly disrupted the ethnic pattern of landholdings. Most obvious are the results of Kenyatta's land resettlement policy, which sought to show tangible fruits of independence in a highly visible way. It also contributed a specific ethnic dimension to the land question: Kenyatta's policy primarily benefited the Kikuyu, who comprised the bulk of new settlers in the Rift Valley, formerly populated by Masai and Kalenjin. This made a significant impact on the distribution of land assets in favour of disadvantaged landless Kikuyu, who made purchases through land-buying companies; and "bourgeois" (mainly Kikuyu) Africans such as civil servants in a position (given literacy and information) to access government mortgages to make individual purchases. Change in the ethnic patterns of land ownership occurred on a remarkable scale and with remarkable speed. As population pressures increased, particularly in Central province, mostly Kikuyu cultivators moved onto lands used by pastoralists, typically through individual purchases. One million Kikuyu settled amidst the Kalenjin in the Rift Valley. The Masai lands have shrunk substantially.

The expectation that granting individual titles, following adjudication and registration, would lessen land disputes was fulfilled in places, according to surveys done in Mbere (Hunt, 1996); but other studies have found increased disputation (Kanyinga, 1996, pp. 12-13). Shipton (1988) notes how adjudication in Nyanza led to deterioration of community relations and ethnic rivalries over land between host and immigrant communities. In the early 1980s, the World Bank noted "already some friction between landless Kikuyu and others who have tried to settle and lay claim to land parcels belonging to some of the pastoral groups" (World Bank, 1983b, p. 19). As in Uganda, family, interpersonal, and interclan quarrels, and envy within ethnic groups, arise from attempts to gain control of former communal land (Hunt, 1996). Such social conflicts have been a primary factor slowing down land adjudication (World Bank, 1983b).

To summarise, land does not seem an important factor in the major violent conflicts in Uganda, which have essentially taken inter-regional and inter-ethnic form. Significant differences from Rwanda include Uganda's considerably lower population density and the tendency towards ethnic homogeneity of the rural population in much of the country. Nonetheless, land has proved an element in some of the Ugandan conflicts. The *Mailo* system of land tenure, which allocated privileges over land to certain Protestant chiefs in Buganda, operated as a source of tension within Buganda occasionally leading to peasant riots, while Amin's 1975 land decree, which essentially abolished some of the *Mailo* privileges, aroused the hostility of the Buganda to Amin and led to their support for the opposition forces in 1979. In contrast, land was a critical dimension of the Rift Valley disturbances in Kenya in the 1990s. The pattern of agricultural development and individualisation of title associated with significant labour mobility, particularly by the Kikuyu, appears to have caused resentment in host areas. Ironically, one key factor in establishing a smallholder class with vested interests in stability in Kenya has in turn sown the seeds for instability.

Economic Integration, Private Sector Development and Social Structure

The degree of integration in an economy affects the incentives for conflict because it determines how much people will lose by the breakdown in the economic system likely to follow from violent conflict. This applies to all income groups, although low-income groups would face smaller potential losses because they have less to lose. The more integrated an economy and the greater the proportionate size of a prosperous middle class, the less the economic motivation for conflict. Kenya and Uganda showed important differences in these respects initially and especially as time passed, as the economic collapse that accompanied violence in Uganda further reduced economic integration and increased the size of the subsistence sector, while Kenya's economy increased integration and established a sizeable middle class.

Economic integration has no single indicator. Table 4.16 compares Kenya and Uganda using a number of measures, all showing greater integration in Kenya especially over time. Uganda started with lower levels of integration, further reduced in response to conflict. The size of the subsistence sector in relation to national income provides the most obvious sign of lack of integration. In Uganda, it reached an estimated 30 per cent of GDP and nearly 60 per cent of agricultural output in 1970. Green (1981) estimated that subsistence income rose to over 40 per cent of GDP and over half of agricultural production in 1980[10]. The shares in Kenya were smaller in 1970 and have diminished since then.

Agricultural activity can provide a fallback in the event of conflict. Uganda generated over half its national income from agriculture in 1960 and the proportion rose sharply during the Amin era, to three-quarters in 1980, more than double agriculture's share in Kenyan GDP. In 1960, nearly nine out of ten Ugandans worked in agriculture, mostly farming their own land and consequently able to switch into subsistence crops if markets collapsed. Over 80 per cent of people in the North produced mainly for subsistence throughout the period (Berg-Schlosser and Siegler, 1990, p. 108).

Table 4.16. **Measures of Economic Integration, Uganda and Kenya**

Measure	Year	Uganda	Kenya
Non-Monetary GDP as Percentage of Total	1970	30.0	
	1980	43.0[a]	
	1986	35.8	
	1995	26.5	
Non-Monetary Agriculture as Percentage of Total Agriculture	1970	59.1	
	1986	56.0	
	1995	46.8	
Agriculture as Percentage of GDP	1960	52	38
	1970	52	33
	1980	76	34
	1985	55	31
	1994	53[b]	28
Industry as Percentage of GDP	1960	13	18
	1970	10	20
	1985	5[c]	21
	1993	12	18
Percentage of Working Population in Agriculture	1960	89	86
	1970	86	82
	1980	83	78
Exports as Percentage of GDP	1970	22	30
	1993	5	42
Primary Exports as Percentage of Total	1965	100	94
	1980	100	84
	1987	100	83
	1993	96	N/A
Road Density: Km. per Million People	1992	118	324
Telephones per Thousand People	1982	2	8
Government Expenditures as Percentage of GDP	1972	22	21
	1980	6	27
	1986	11	25
	1994	20	30
Social and Economic Expenditures as Percentage of GDP	1972	8.9	13.4
	1980	2.1	14.4
	1986	3.9	13.5
	1994	4.8	11.7

Notes: *a)* Calculated by Green (1981), allocating the *magendo* economy (illegal monetary and subsistence activity) to the monetary and subsistence sectors. Green estimates that in 1980 the economy was 26 per cent subsistence, 24 per cent monetary (legal) and 51 per cent *magendo*; *b)* 1993; *c)* 1987.

Sources: World Bank, *World Development Reports*; World Bank (1996*a*); Republic of Uganda (1996*b*).

In Kenya, variations in the contribution of different provinces to total marketed production indicate differing degrees of integration into the national economy. In the early 1970s, the Rift Valley dominated in cereals, tea and livestock, and Central province dominated coffee output. Most provinces made a significant contribution to marketed output relative to their share of population. Yet one should not overstate the extent of economic integration in Kenya. Indicators such as access to markets and transport suggest that most people across the country are fairly well integrated into the national economy, but most provinces market little agricultural output and participation in off-farm employment is limited (below 10 per cent everywhere except Nairobi and Central province) (Table 4.17).

Table 4.17. **Market Integration in Kenya by Province**

Province	Provincial Shares of Marketed Output, 1971-72		Per Cent of Work Force Employed in Official Forms of Employment[a]	Per Cent of Population less than Two Miles to Market
	Cereals	Coffee		
Central	12.3	74.6	11.3	41.7
Coast	0	0.1	9.8	22.4
Eastern	5.5	15.4	8.9	25.3
Nyanza	3.2	4.1	5.1	46.3
Rift Valley	62.7	4.7	9.1	34.9
Western	16.3	1.1	12.6	38.4
Northeast	0	0	N/A	N/A
Nairobi	0	0	N/A	N/A
National	100.0	100.0	9.2	37.1

Note: a) Including government.
Sources: Bigsten (1977), pp. 18-20; Republic of Kenya, *Statistical Abstract 1981*.

In Uganda, the lower proportion of output exported and the very high proportion of exports accounted for by primary products involving relatively little domestic processing also indicate relatively little economic integration. Kenya's industrial sector, which in an import-substituting regime tends to have fairly strong connections with the rest of the economy for markets, was substantially larger than Uganda's in 1970, at around a fifth of GDP compared to only 10 per cent (dropping to as low as 5 per cent in 1987) in Uganda. Urbanisation proceeded much farther in Kenya than Uganda from similar starting points at independence. In 1993, more than one in four Kenyans were urban residents, compared to only just over one in ten in Uganda. Data for road and telephone density (Table 4.16) show Uganda behind Kenya, with among the lowest ratios in the world in 1992. Government provision of social and economic services, another important dimension, determines how much citizens might lose if services were withdrawn. Kenya has devoted much more of national income to such services.

Greater economic integration broadly reflects how economic development, modernisation and the penetration of the market have gone farther in Kenya, along with quite vigorous development of the small- medium- and large-scale private sector. From the outset, recognition of the principle of private property and an emphasis upon economic growth formed the hallmarks of the Kenyan approach to development. In 1992, the World Bank described Kenya as having "the most diversified structure of private enterprise in Africa" (World Bank, 1992a, p. 3). In agriculture, the mainstay of the Kenyan economy, the share of small farms in marketed production increased markedly over the first decade, from 22 per cent to 52 per cent (Lele and Meyers, 1989).

Both the industrial and agricultural private sectors received strong state support in the form of subsidies and other policies. Examples of interventions designed to increase Kenyanisation of the economy and promote private sector development include the Industrial Development and Commercial Corporation, industrial estates and the Industrial Development Bank. The industrial estates programme for small manufacturers, established in major and secondary towns and associated with the geographical spread of industrial activity, has been regarded as relatively successful. Development financing institutions tended to favour larger and often already successful business operations despite a high incidence of loan default[11].

Public institutions dominated the marketing of agricultural commodities in Kenya, with marketing boards for grain, coffee, tea and sugar. Subsidies were provided through controls on input prices (such as fertiliser) and guaranteed purchase of output at prices close to international levels. In general, however, the government structured interventions mainly to benefit larger-scale producers[12].

Kenya had considerable social and economic mobility. Development created substantial economic opportunities for a growing African middle class, with a symbiosis between the state and the private sector. This class, together with its employees and the more prosperous medium-scale entrepreneurs and farmers and their employees, gained a strong economic interest in continued political stability.

In contrast, Uganda did not place the same emphasis on private sector development in the 1960s. Economic opportunities outside the state existed for Southerners, but Northerners had few and saw the best way to gain higher incomes as through the state. They therefore were determined to secure and maintain control over the state and prevent Southerners' dominating there as they did elsewhere. When Amin gained control, his "Economic War" against the Asians and Europeans released assets and positions which he gave largely to his own people. Other groups lost badly during his regime. Drastic cuts in real wages in the 1970s accounted for disaffection of urban workers (Jamal, 1991). The collapse of the marketing network and huge reductions in prices paid to farmers decimated the incomes of large- and medium-scale farmers (Fendru, 1985). Very limited entrepreneurial or private-sector opportunities meant that control of access to the state became all-important for the prosperity of the middle classes.

The two countries' social structures reflect their different profiles of development. The estimates in Table 4.17 show some similarities and some important differences. Among the key differences, Kenya had significantly more capitalists and urban formal sector workers than Uganda in 1980. While the total proportion of people in farming was lower in Kenya than Uganda by 1980 — 67 per cent as against 83 per cent — Kenya had relatively more middle-size farmers, nearly a quarter of its agriculturalists as against 13.5 per cent in Uganda. The figures presented by Berg-Schlosser and Siegler suggest the growing relative importance of the Kenyan middle class over the period 1960-80 (Table 4.18). The share of the male workforce falling into the categories of managers, non-agrarian *petite bourgeoisie*, salariat and the state class (elite) expanded significantly up to 1980. Since the mid-1980s, however, such trends as the erosion of civil service conditions and retrenchment, as well as rising unemployment among educated youth, have probably affected the size and sense of well-being of the middle class in Kenya.

Table 4.18. **Social Structures: Uganda, Kenya and Tanzania**

Per Cent of Male Workforce	Uganda	Kenya		Tanzania	
	1980	1960[a]	1980	1967	1980
State Employees and Salariat[b]	7.0	5.4 (2.7)	8.1	2.4	3.1
Capitalists[c]	0.006	0.2	0.14	0.3	0.8[d]
Urban Workers, Formal Sector	3.5	12.5 (12.3)	15.0	9.4	7.2
Urban Workers, Informal Sector[e]	6.1	1.1	6.6	7.3	13.9
Large-scale Farmers	0.3	0.1	0.04	0.05[f]	0.01[f]
Medium-scale Farmers	11.2	5.3	15.8	6.7	4.6
Small Farmers	68.8	63.9 (63.9)	42.3	69.1	67.6
Landless Farm Workers	2.6	9.5 (9.5)	8.8	4.5	2.2

Notes: a) Figures in brackets are for Africans; b) employed mainly by the state; c) includes managers only; d) Zanzibar only; e) Includes workers, entrepreneurs and the self-employed; f) Mainland only.

Source: Berg-Schlosser and Siegler (1990).

Kenya was almost unique among African states in creating, at an early stage of nationhood, a middle class with an aversion to disruptive change. This outcome had in fact been an explicit objective of the colonial authorities. The expansion of private land ownership, cash-cropping and formal-sector job opportunities, partly through the high growth of the civil service until the mid-1980s, as well as advances in secondary and university education, all provided a base for a reasonably diverse middle class. Strong urban-rural links, especially *via* remittances, spread the benefits widely. Some of these developments occurred in Uganda in the 1960s, but as the economy stagnated during the Amin and Obote II conflicts, the likely economic or social gains from supporting government stability eroded, while the potential rewards from overthrowing the regime, taking control of the state and restoring stability increased. Ambitious leaders had much to reap from controlling state levers of power; their followers, chiefly the peasantry, had little to lose.

One should not neglect those groups which have not shared in Kenya's past growth. This analysis already has looked at trends in the incidence and location of poverty. Kenya has significant numbers of disenfranchised youth, given high rates of unemployment especially among secondary school graduates. It has a young population — about half the total population is under 15 — for which the earlier period of economic prosperity and nation-building has little relevance. This, together with the economic stagnation of recent years and the uncertainties associated with the transition to multiparty rule, could provide the basis for unrest in the future. In this sense, the continuing tension and outbreaks of violence throughout much of 1997 bode ill for the future.

Notes

1. This is also the view of Humphreys (1996) after examining a number of countries in conflict.

2. The "southern" part of Uganda is to be understood as including the Central and Western regions, while the "northern" part normally includes both the Northern and Eastern regions.

3. In 1989, user fees were introduced for outpatient and inpatient services. Despite the waivers provided for those unable to pay, evidence suggests that the charges have negatively affected access by the poor to health services.

4. As noted, however, the concentration of formal managerial and professional employment in Central region might be expected given the location of the capital there.

5. The data for the early period and the 1990s come from completely different sources and this may well account for some or all of the change.

6. Unfortunately, variations in provincial prices are neglected here. It is obviously likely that the cost of living is higher in urban areas, for rent and transport as well as food. Yet the conclusions here regarding average per capita income are consistent with the finding of significantly lower incidence of poverty in urban areas (in 1992, 29.3 per cent by head count, versus 46.4 per cent in rural areas).

7. The result for Northeastern province is most surprising, but is based on the same source.

8. Lecturer in the Faculty of Law at Makerere.

9. This includes land that is inadequate in quality as well as quantity, which may explain the apparent contradiction.

10. Green (1981) estimates that the subsistence economy together with the *magendo* economy — the illegal non-official monetary economy — accounted for over three-quarters of national income in 1980 (Green, 1981).

11. See Njuguna, 1995.

12. For grain, Ikiara *et al.* (1995) found that most small-scale growers in 1993 sold to private traders, not to the state, mainly because they could not afford the delays involved in dealing with the government agencies.

Chapter 5

Costs and Benefits of Conflict:
A Summary

To aid the exposition, this chapter employs a set of simple matrices which highlight and summarise the costs and benefits of conflict to various groups. These usefully summarise the impact of the various economic and social influences analysed in the previous chapters.

— The eruption of conflict requires agreement among leaders, often from the elite, and followers who come from lower income categories. Thus one needs to evaluate the relative costs and benefits of different socio-economic groups within the same ethno-regional group.

— The prospects for conflict can depend importantly on how the size of different groups has changed over time. Note, for example, the increasing absolute and relative numbers of the poor and very poor in Kenya since the 1980s.

— The judgements contained in the matrices clearly are subjective, although derived from information already presented.

— Even given strong incentives for violence, actual action depends partly on the strength of the state and its determination to suppress opposition. A very strong repressive machine may prevent violence.

The matrices clearly represent gross oversimplification. For example, they partition Uganda into only two geographic categories, North and South, each stratified into three socio-economic categories, thus submerging complexities which are clear from the earlier discussion. Kenya's more advanced economic development and socio-economic differentiation require further breakdowns, e.g. distinguishing between the rural and urban middle classes. The following additional points will help the reader to navigate within the matrices.

— Kenya has two matrices, covering the Kenyatta and Moi regimes. This abstracts from changes that took place during each of them. Possible alternative specifications could, for example, distinguish the post-1992 period of multipartyism. For Uganda, the post-independence period has been divided into four subperiods broadly illustrative of underlying changes, the eras of Obote I and II, Amin and Museveni.

— Any economic cost/benefit calculus must include the costs of disruption as well as the potential gains from winning a conflict, the latter being only possibilities, not certainties.

Table 5.1. **Kenya and Uganda:**
Costs and Benefits of Conflict as Perceived by Different Groups

A. Kenya: The Kenyatta Period

Group	Costs of Conflict			Potential Gains from Conflict		
	Economic Disruption and Lost Income	Lost Access to State Services	Loss of Life and Property	Access to State Benefits	Appropriation of Land and Property	Access to Decision-making Organs
Elite						
Kikuyu	high	high	high	high	low	low
Kalenjin	n.r.	moderate	moderate	low	moderate	moderate
Middle Class						
Urban	high	high	high	high	low	low
Rural	high	high	high	high	low	low
Poor						
Urban	low	low	low	moderate	moderate	moderate
Unempl. Youth	n.r.	n.r.	low	low	moderate	moderate
Rural Poor:						
Kalenjin	low/n.r.	low/n.r.	low	low	moderate	moderate
Kikuyu	low	low	low	moderate	low	low
Very Poor						
Urban	low	low	low	low	moderate	moderate
Rural	low	low	low	low	moderate	moderate
Kenyan Asians/Whites	high	mod. - high	high	high	very low	mod. - low

B. Kenya: The Moi Period

Group	Costs of Conflict			Potential Gains from Conflict		
	Economic Disruption	Loss of Access to State Services	Loss of Life and Property	Access to State Benefits	Appropriation of Land and Property	Access to Decision-making Organs
Elite						
Kikuyu	high	high	high	low	low	moderate
Kalenjin	high	high	high	high	moderate	low
Middle Class						
Rural	moderate	moderate	moderate	moderate	low	moderate
Urban	moderate	moderate	moderate	moderate	low	moderate
Poor						
Urban	low	low	low	n.r.	moderate	moderate
Unempl. Youth	n.r.	n.r.	low	n.r.	moderate	moderate
Rural Poor:						
Kalenjin	low	low	low	low	low	low
Kikuyu	low	low	low	high	low	moderate
Isolated	low	low	low	low	high	low
Very Poor						
Urban	low	n.r.	low	n.r.	moderate	moderate
Rural	n.r.	n.r.	low	n.r.	moderate	moderate
Kenyan Asians/Whites	high	high	high	high	low	moderate

62

Table 5.1 (continued)

C. Uganda: Obote I, 1962-70

Groups	Costs of Conflict		Potential Gains from Conflict		
	Disrupted Markets/Lost Incomes	Lost Access to State Benefits	Control over Government Decisions	Jobs and Higher Incomes	Projects
North					
Elite	high	moderate	0	0	0
Middle	moderate	moderate	0	0	0
Low	low	moderate	0	0	0
South					
Elite	high	moderate	high	high	high
Middle	high	moderate	0	moderate	high
Low	high	moderate	0	0	moderate

D. Uganda: Amin, 1971-79

Groups	Costs of Conflict		Potential Gains from Conflict			
	Disrupted Markets/Lost Incomes	Lost Access to State Benefits	Control over Government Decisions		Jobs and Higher Incomes	Projects
			West Nubians	Others		
North						
Elite	low	low	0	high	moderate	moderate
Middle	low	low	0	0	moderate	moderate
Low	low	low	0	0	moderate	moderate
South						
Elite	very low	very low	high		moderate	moderate
Middle	very low	very low	0		moderate	moderate
Low	very low	very low	0		moderate	moderate

E. Uganda: Obote II, 1980-85

Groups	Costs of Conflict		Potential Gains from Conflict		
	Disrupted Markets/Lost Incomes	Lost Access to State Benefits	Control over Government Decisions	Jobs and Higher Incomes	Projects
North					
Elite	moderate	low	0	0	moderate
Middle	moderate	low	0	moderate	moderate
Low	low	low	0	moderate	moderate
South					
Elite	moderate	very low	high	high	moderate
Middle	low	very low	0	moderate	moderate
Low	low	very low	0	moderate	moderate

F. Uganda: Museveni, 1986-97

Groups	Costs of Conflict		Potential Gains from Conflict		
	Disrupted Markets/Lost Incomes	Lost Access to State Benefits	Control over Government Decisions	Jobs and Higher Incomes	Projects
North					
Elite	moderate	moderate	moderate	low	low
Middle	moderate	low	0	low	low
Low	low	low	0	low	low
South					
Elite	high	moderate	low	very low	very low
Middle	high	moderate	0	very low	very low
Low	high	moderate	0	very low	very low

Notes: n.r. = not relevant; West Nubians: from Amin's area.
Source: Authors' own calculations, from previous text and tables.

63

The matrices reveal that the costs of conflict have tended to predominate over the perceived benefits in Kenya, but in Uganda the calculus has clearly favoured peace only during periods of relative economic prosperity. Amin's own desire for power motivated his coup, but many groups welcomed it although they would not have instigated it, because they had not shared in the fruits of development during Obote I (Mudoola, 1992). Towards the end of the Amin era, economic disruptions had become so great that most groups had little to lose by conflict, while the potential gains appeared high.

The start of Obote's second period of office saw an economic recovery and, initially at least, the perceived economic costs of conflict tended to increase; but because participation in the legal monetary economy remained very low and the Amin legacy had left state services and benefits nearly negligible, the costs of conflict had fallen. As the rebel forces gained ground, Obote retaliated, conflict erupted, immense economic disruption arose again, especially in the Luwero Triangle, and once again the potential net gains of the elite and others in the South favoured conflict in order to re-establish order.

The Museveni decade has seen a much more firmly based recovery of the economy and some restoration of state services and benefits, law and order reinstated and power, jobs and projects more widely shared[1]. The calculus has changed to favour continuing peace. It now suggests that the North would lose more from conflict than it gained from peace, even if the gains are low due to the high levels of poverty that persist. In 1993, a boom in prices for sim-sim — a crop important in this area — greatly improved economic opportunities and the fighting virtually ceased, only to resume when prices fell again. Conflict has nonetheless persisted in the North despite the small gains it offers; its leaders seek power for themselves and they secure support from villagers through inducements and terror[2]. They survive in part through foreign support.

The relative costs and benefit from conflicts differ among socio-economic groups as is illustrated below.

The Poor

During the first decade after independence in both countries the incidence of poverty fell and access to social services and prospects for upward mobility improved. Hence the costs of conflict during this period were generally moderate to high in both countries, with the exception of Uganda's North and Kenya's Northeast, where prospects of disrupted markets and services had much less relevance. The Kikuyu peasantry and low-income groups in Uganda's South had more interest in stability at that time, relative to "peripheral" groups with less access to state resources, economic opportunities and political structures.

The perceived costs and benefits of conflict differed significantly between the poor and very poor in Kenya; but for Uganda, much more limited overall access to public services and benefits rendered the calculus of the poor similar to that of Kenya's very poor. Strikingly, many of the potential costs of conflict are either not relevant or not present for both categories. For example, disrupted access to health care or state benefits has little meaning to those who never benefited from them.

Notwithstanding a lack of data for Uganda, poverty undoubtedly rose when average incomes fell, although the very poor in the subsistence sector remained relatively unaffected. Evidence exists of rising poverty in Uganda in recent years. A steep rise in the absolute and relative numbers of poor in Kenya over the past two decades has made their perceptions potentially far more potent. There were greater numbers of people in severe poverty in the Moi period than under Kenyatta. Available evidence suggests that the poor themselves feel their material welfare has significantly diminished over the years from 1985. "Ten years ago we had a crop in the field, a well-stocked granary, a cow. Today, because of land subdivision, high prices of seeds and fertiliser, we have small and patchy yields, the granaries are empty, the cows have been sold, and we rely on government relief food" (UNICEF/ODA/AMREF, 1995, p. vii).

The Kenyan matrices distinguish unemployed youth as a separate category. They focus on the male unemployed in urban areas, on the assumption that they make up the most potent group for potential conflict. Among youth, the costs of disruption to the *status quo* appear low. Indeed increasing levels of criminality indicate such sentiments. Here also, many of the potential costs of conflict, such as disruption to market activity, do not apply and weigh less heavily in conflict deterrence. This group may also see potential gains, beyond immediate appropriation of property, in future access to land. In Kenya, personal criminal violence has risen steadily; dissatisfaction has been expressed through this increased rate of crime against persons and property, rather than more systematic and cohesive group-based conflict.

Isolated Communities

Among the isolated communities, especially their poor, several factors in the individual calculus of the costs and benefits of conflict become irrelevant. In Uganda, after the first decade of independence, the elite and poor alike tended to perceive very low economic costs of conflict. This became particularly marked during the Amin era but has changed only slowly over time, persisting even into the Museveni regime for many in the North and West.

While indicators such as access to markets and transport for Kenya suggest that most people across the country are fairly well-integrated into the national economy, Northeast province markets little agricultural output (other than livestock) and participates little in formal sector employment. Local conflict prevails in the isolated Northeastern province, motivated by the prospects of short-term economic gain amidst widespread poverty and deprivation, a situation not unlike the downward spiral of underdevelopment and conflict that has characterised Uganda. Heavily armed, marauding bands seeking livestock as well as access to water have created insecurity which has become the greatest hindrance to development in the province (Maalim, 1995).

The Middle Class

The middle class in Kenya has played a relatively important role, in both its size and its effect on regime stability. Its calculus in both the Kenyatta and Moi periods resembled that of the ruling elites in Uganda. While their benefits accrue on a smaller scale than those of the elites, both the urban and rural middle classes clearly face potentially significant costs from conflict. The express objective of the colonial Swynnerton Plan to create a Kenyan commercial class on the land with a vested interest in stability and the establishment of a "politically stable community" has been fulfilled (Swynnerton, 1955, p. 10, cited in Hunt, 1996).

The Economic and Political Elites

The calculus of costs and benefits portrayed in the matrices assumes gains from capturing the state, because the group controlling the state monopolises its resources. Outsiders may perceive potential gains from such a capture, but in general and regardless of affiliation, the elites would tend to suffer the costs of disruption and fear damage to their property. The degree of development of the private sector governs this view. In Kenya, even where the elites are excluded from state employment, the costs of market disruption may still hold sway. The Kikuyu during the Moi period have seen the costs of market disruption as more significant for them than the perceived gains associated with the seizure of state structures, a consequence more likely in the wake of economic liberalisation. Limited development in Uganda meant that the paucity of alternative sources of income outside the state increased the potential gains from conflict. The southern elite during the first Obote period saw such gains as high, and they remained significant until Museveni came to power and the fruits of economic recovery and growth became evident. During the Amin era, elites from both the North and South perceived real gains from conflict, which had devastating consequences for all of Uganda.

Kenyan Asians and Whites

The Asian and white communities perceived overwhelmingly negative repercussions of conflict. The Amin era in Uganda bore this out. To the extent that these groups have access (albeit limited) to political decision-making structures, they would tend to have a stabilising influence. This probably has occurred in Kenya. On the other hand, while the relative and absolute sizes of these groups have diminished significantly, they retain considerable, conspicuous economic and financial power which has created resentment among other Kenyan groups; this resentment has come to the fore against Asians in particular and in violent crime.

Constraints on Opposition[3]

Even when the economic gains from conflict outweigh the costs, conflict does not necessarily follow. The outcome depends on both consensual and non-consensual aspects. The former include opportunities for political participation and peaceful change. The Kenyan system even during the one-party period provided considerable opportunities for participation and local voice, for example through the election and frequent turnover of local parliamentarians, although not for a change in the regime as a whole.

The range of available instruments whose use or threat may effectively constrain conflict show striking similarities in Kenya and Uganda — a fact partially attributable to their common colonial heritage. Both have had a significant centralisation of power in the office of the President. The major distinction between them lies in the extent to which their regimes have chosen to use their powers of repression. The differences arose in part from the predilections of individual leaders, but also from sharp political fault lines present in Uganda. The common elements that form the potential basis for repression fall broadly under the headings of repressive legislation and state security operations.

The Repressive Corpus of Public Law

Before independence, Africans in Uganda had criticised the virtually unfettered powers of the police and the original Ugandan constitution included a Bill of Rights. Kenyan nationalists pledged to eliminate the laws which facilitated human rights abuses during the colonial period. The 1961 election manifesto of KANU referred specifically to the *Preservation of Public Security Ordinance* and detention without trial as unjust and arbitrary (Oloka-Onyango, 1990, p. 15). Yet in both countries the framework for repression has remained.

Ugandans saw civil liberties curtailed from about 1965. The *1965 Police (Amendment) Act* gave the Inspector General unlimited power to prohibit assemblies likely to cause a breach of the peace; in 1966, opposition parties were banned and a State of Emergency declared. Detention without trial became common; between 1966 and 1971 the *Uganda Gazette* listed over 500 people as having been arrested under the provisions of the Emergency Regulations, not including those arrested for less than four weeks or on remand. During the first rule of Obote, there were several judicial findings of illegal government detention, but the government circumvented them through legislative amendment. Amin vested judicial powers in the Military Tribunal, the Defence Council and the "Economic Crimes" Tribunal, effectively removing any pretence at judicial independence.

Museveni brought limited improvements, cleaning up the armed forces and instituting new laws to protect citizens against arbitrary detention. A new office of Inspector General of Government had the duty of protecting and promoting human rights and the rule of law. The *Security Organisation Statute* gave the intelligence agencies a statutory basis for the first time. The Human Rights Commission set up in 1986 enquired into all aspects of human rights abuses from 1962 to 1986. Nevertheless, other laws have extended government powers, e.g. by broadening the definition of "police officer" to any member of the NRM, while retaining the repressive *Public Order and Security Act of 1967* (Khiddu-Makabuya, 1989). Political parties could not participate in elections.

The most notorious pieces of Kenyan legislation that repress potential opposition to the regime include:

— The *Preservation of Public Security Act* grants extensive presidential powers including detention without trial.

— The *Public Order Act* prevents assembly without previous written permission.

— The *Societies Act* prohibits any association of more than nine citizens without permission; the *NGO Co-ordination Act* regulates any political activity, as does the *Co-operative Societies Act*.

— The *Penal Code* contains an extraordinarily widely defined offence of sedition (Nowrojee, 1993).

— The *Chiefs Act* gives extensive powers to these presidential appointees to affect people's daily lives. The structure of provincial administration in Kenya created the chief as a local agent of the central (originally colonial) authorities although, in contrast to Uganda, the system had not fully developed during colonisation. Now the chiefs and local security committees report to the Office of the President, leaving little local autonomy.

State Security Agencies

Extensive police powers in Kenya and Uganda trace directly to colonial ordinances and practices. From the outset, the police had paramilitary powers of enforcement (Oloka-Onyango, 1990). Many of the extraordinary powers vested in the force to deal with the *Mau Mau* insurgency became entrenched during the emergency declared by Kenyatta in 1966 and in force until 1982.

In Kenya, however, repression has extended far less than in Uganda, where the armed forces have played a pivotal role. As early as 1964, the General Service Unit (GSU) and a presidential guard known as the Special Police Force (SPF), which extended the repressive authority of the government, reinforced the Ugandan police[4]. The army grew after the mutinies of 1964 and played an increasingly political role during Obote I, especially after 1966. When Amin, himself the army commander, seized power in 1971, he repealed Obote's State of Emergency but simultaneously banned all political activity, vesting supreme power in himself. Military and quasi-military forces usurped the police. They were given extensive powers of arrest. The reign of terror that followed included the brutal and arbitrary actions of the State Research Bureau, the Public Safety Unit and Military Intelligence. The State Research Bureau, the hub of Amin's power, comprised 3 000 men, mainly Moslems or non-Ugandans, "dressed incognito in flowered shirts, bell-bottom trousers, sunglasses and platform shoes ... notorious for tossing their victims into the trunks of their cars ... the victims were never seen alive again" (Avirgan and Honey, 1982, quoted in Khiddu-Makabuya, 1989, p. 148).

The military retained dominant powers from 1980 to 1986, with no reconstruction of the police, and an emergent "new repressive apparatus". Factionalism in the government reproduced itself inside the army and intelligence services (Mamdani, 1988). Obote II instituted a number of new government agencies to establish "law and order", including the National Security Agency (NASA) and a reconstituted Special Police Force. These forces now dominated, abusing human rights by arbitrary arrest, detention, torture etc. NASA became particularly notorious for its abuses in the Luwero Triangle[5].

A major objective of the Museveni regime was to recruit a "nationally balanced" army, police and local defence forces with professional codes of conduct. Local Resistance Councils (a new form of local political institution) were given a role in matters of law and order. The armed forces' Code of Conduct made it an offence for any soldier to abuse, insult or molest a civilian, with penalties of execution or imprisonment (Republic of Uganda, NRM Secretariat, 1987). The restructured police force excluded any who had abused human rights or fell below a minimum educational standard; initially only 3 000 out of 22 000 remained, but subsequent recruitment brought the ranks of police (plus prison officers) to 26 000 in January 1995. Abuses have continued during the war in the North, however. For example, Amnesty International noted the detention without trial of over 4 000 alleged political opponents in the North and Northeast in 1988 and 1989. The numbers fell thereafter but incidents of torture, ill-treatment in custody and the killing of civilians continued to be reported[6].

Kenya's state security operations have been less overt and brutal but nonetheless extensive. Security enforcement occurs in part through the provincial administrations, down to the chiefs and sub-chiefs who form security committees that report on anti-state behaviour. At the national level, the armed forces and in particular the paramilitary General Services Unit play an important role in enforcing domestic stability. Intimidation and physical torture of opposition activists appears to be on the rise, as evidenced by the shocking treatment of the falsely accused Ndeiya Six (*Africa Confidential*, Vol. 35, No. 14).

In Kenya, the police rather than the army have acted as the preferred instrument of repression. The Kenyan Human Rights Commission's *Quarterly Repression Reports* contain chapters on police brutality, inhumane treatment, arbitrary arrests and irregular detentions, reporting dozens of such cases each month. Table 3.1 (page 21) presented the numbers on reported police harassment of the poor in recent years. The organs dealing with security and political intelligence, which evolved into today's Special Branch, have been the most brutal and violent. Police officers, as agents of the President, enjoy virtually unfettered powers of arrest and detention, and the judiciary has done little to protect individual rights in this context. Kenya's geographic and demographic diversity has influenced the operation of this security framework. While Northeastern province faces more repressive rules as a legacy of the Shifta war, governmental authorities exert little effective restraint on banditry and raids.

This review indicates that government powers have been strong throughout in both Kenya and Uganda and in principle might have been expected to act as a restraint against both legitimate and violent opposition. This seems to have occurred in Kenya albeit in a context with significantly lower incentives for violent opposition than in Uganda. In Uganda the very extensive, arbitrary and despotic nature of state powers, and especially the repression of peaceful political opposition, were used to initiate and provoke violence. The state instigated much of the violence of Obote I, Amin and a good deal of Obote II; the strength of its machinery served to increase violence rather than repress it. In every regime, perhaps including the Museveni one, it seems that violence offers the only possible path to secure power, while government abuses, significantly less in the Museveni regime but still present especially in the North, increase the incentive to remove the source of such abuses by overthrowing the regime.

External Influences

While external influences have not been given explicit consideration in this study of the motivations for conflict in East Africa, foreign intervention and finance have indeed played a role. During each of the conflicts in Uganda, antigovernment fighters secured financial support and arms supplies from a range of international partners, who did not cause but greatly facilitated their efforts. Uganda stands apart from Kenya, where the only alleged foreign involvement in opposition movements came from Somalia during the Shifta wars. However, until the early 1990s, Kenya received significant financial and military support from Western donors which helped to promote stability. There does not appear to have been external support for politically destabilising forces in Tanzania, which received relatively large amounts of development aid for most of its post-independence history. Tanzania's own support for liberation movements elsewhere in the region imposed heavy economic costs, however.

The Amin coup is believed to have had the support and possibly help of the Israelis and the British, who had been antagonised by Obote's economic and foreign policies. Britain was the first country to recognise the new regime (Furley, 1989), which other industrialised countries also welcomed. Members of Amin's notorious State Research Bureau are believed to have received basic training in the United Kingdom and the United States (Khiddu-Makabuya, 1989). After the wholesale murder of Acholi and Langi troops and the expulsion of Asians, the United Kingdom halted its aid and stopped trade officially, but British firms continued to supply goods on the "whisky run", which provided luxury goods and equipment. US trade expanded until an embargo was declared in 1978 as evidence of Amin's atrocities accumulated. Libya and other Middle Eastern countries replaced Western support after Amin expelled the

Israelis. Eastern bloc countries provided training and supplies for the army (Furley, 1989). Throughout the Amin regime, the Tanzanian government continued to support Obote and opposition forces; they helped launch an unsuccessful attack on Amin in 1972, and the subsequent successful attack in 1978-79 included substantial Tanzanian forces.

Tanzania strongly supported Obote and is widely believed to have been instrumental in getting him reinstated. Obote also received widespread support in the West, with the British leading a move to write off Uganda's debts and provide additional aid. Western and multilateral aid to Uganda resumed. The British continued to support Obote and train troops even after the growing evidence of atrocities reported by Amnesty International, which led to the withdrawal of US support. The British began to reconsider their position only on Amnesty's publication of *Uganda Six Years after Amin* in 1985.

Museveni's NRM had little external support at first, but once in power he gained widespread international support. He started with a handful of soldiers and secured arms from successful attacks on army camps. People of the Western region and Buganda provided food and men, largely without cost. He is believed to have received some arms and financial support from Libya.

Support from neighbouring countries has helped the movements opposing Museveni. The West Nile Bank Movement received support from Zaire, in retaliation for support for Zairian opposition forces and refugees in Uganda. The Christian rebels in the North have been helped by finance and arms from Sudan, partly because Uganda's government has supported the opposition against the Sudanese government in southern Sudan.

Kenya has attracted significantly more foreign investment than Uganda. Nairobi became the East African base for a number of multinational corporations, attracted by the country's openness to foreign investment and its relative stability. For much of the period, Kenya remained one of very few African countries with a pro-Western outlook while Soviet influence became evident in many of its neighbours. In the terms of the cost-benefit calculus used in this study, the costs of conflict for Western interests (disruption to markets and loss of property and possibly life) outweighed the benefits by far. The West had a vested interest in the continuation of the *status quo* in Kenya and showed it through generous levels of aid, plus military support when coups were threatened (as in 1964 and 1982).

The situation of Kenya *vis à vis* the West changed somewhat in the early 1990s. Employing such levers as the temporary suspension of international financial assistance, the Western donor community put substantial pressure on the Moi government to move to multipartyism, even at the risk of ethnic conflict. The multiparty elections probably would not have occurred without foreign pressure. Supporters of the Moi regime might argue that the ethnic clashes before each election would not have erupted if the elections had not been announced (and by implication if the West had not interfered). The Western stance might be explained by arguing that the end of the Soviet presence may have rendered Kenya's stability expendable.

Immediately after independence in Tanzania, disputes over issues such as its[7] recognition of the German Democratic Republic, its position against Southern Rhodesia's UDI, and its support for the independence movement in Mozambique drove away its three largest Western donors: the USA, the UK and Germany. Although the First Five-Year Development Plan (1964-69) envisaged 78 per cent of investment financing from external sources, 14 per cent from domestic borrowing and 8 per cent from taxation, Tanzania ended up financing 62 per cent of its development spending domestically (Migot-Adholla *in* Barkan, ed., 1984), at the same time as a fall in the price of its main export, sisal, necessitated more foreign aid than initially projected. After the Arusha Declaration and Nyerere's adoption of a non-alignment policy, China became the primary donor in the early 1970s, although its share became insignificant thereafter.

Tanzania obtained highly concessional loans, especially until the mid-1970s, from both the Eastern Bloc and the West, due mainly to its strategic position as a front-line state that managed to maintain a large measure of internal political stability while attempting to strike a balance between socialist ideology and pragmatism — amidst several bordering countries with strong rebel movements. The Arusha Declaration generated the support of the Nordic countries during the 1970s, which helped finance social programmes throughout the decade. These countries played an especially important role in financing infrastructure spending in the first half of the 1970s and productive activities in the second half[8].

Although largely instrumental in establishing industrial and infrastructure facilities, dependence on foreign capital became a major problem after the mid-1970s. In the 1980s, Tanzania became one of the world's leading foreign assistance recipients and the largest recipient per capita in Africa (Gordon *in* Barkan, ed., 1984, p. 305)[9]. When they realised that aid had not effectively increased industrial capacity use or investment efficiency, however, foreign donors, including the Scandinavian countries, either decreased disbursements or switched to commodity support in the mid-1980s. In 1987, for example, the share of commodity support amounted to 44 per cent of total foreign aid (Havnevik *et al.*, 1988, p. 135).

Tanzania allowed China and the USSR to train the guerrilla armies of Mozambique, Angola, Zimbabwe and Namibia on its territory. Its support for these liberation movements as well as for the African National Congress in South Africa cost it a great deal, necessitating strengthened security against incursions by those countries searching for members of the opposition. Support for the anti-Amin forces in 1978 also was costly. War with Uganda increased expenditures on transport and defence from 12.3 per cent of GDP in 1976/77 to 24.4 per cent in 1977/78 (Havnevik *et al.*, 1988, p. 56). The war in Uganda cost Tanzania an estimated $500 million (about 15 per cent of its GNP in 1978) (Gordon *in* Barkan, ed., 1984, p. 326). Defence spending thus increased substantially during the first half and at the end of the 1970s. In 1979, defence reached about 40 per cent of total recurrent spending, a 75 per cent increase over the previous year (Bank of Tanzania, 1983). Tanzania also hosted Rwanda and Burundi refugees, whose numbers increased further after 1993 following the turmoil after the assassination of the two countries' presidents.

On balance, aid donors contributed to political stability in Tanzania and Kenya by helping finance strong expansion in social infrastructure, but the adjustment process which brought about cutbacks in Tanzania after the early 1980s and a slowdown in Kenya in the 1990s have undermined this effect, contributing to potential tensions. In Uganda, external influences did little for peaceful development up to 1986, providing support for Amin and later for Obote, despite their gross human rights abuses. After some hesitation, external aid has made a large contribution to recovery and development during the Museveni era.

Notes

1. Musuveni's first cabinet contained 13 Buganda, 12 southern Bantu and eight from the East and North.

2. "Only a minority of Acholi join the rebels freely. Most LRS recruits are kidnapped children. Unicef ... estimates that 3 000 children have been taken in the past two years alone" (*The Observer*, 5 Jan. 1997).

3. This section draws heavily on Oloka-Onyango (1990).

4. The GSU was composed of poorly educated personnel who "infiltrated all spheres of government and all areas of life ... Many persons who revealed an independence of mind found themselves questioned in degrading circumstances" (Republic of Uganda, 1971*b*, quoted in Khiddu-Makabuya, 1989, p. 146).

5. They were described as the "computer men", getting their nickname from the computer printouts they carried with lists of opposition suspects. "They pick out the 'bandits' or 'dissidents' and take them away. Often these people are never seen again" (*Africa Now*, July 1984, quoted in Khiddu-Makabuya, 1989, p. 151).

6. See successive reports of Amnesty International.

7. More accurately, Zanzibar's.

8. Sweden provided more than 10 per cent of foreign aid to Tanzania in 1979 (Stewart, 1986, p. 99).

9. Between 1982 and 1985, the Nordic countries accounted for about 28.7 per cent of total foreign aid to Tanzania, followed by the EC countries with 20.4 per cent and the World Bank/IDA with 10.6 per cent. The World Bank/IDA loans declined substantially (more than 60 per cent) during this period, probably due to Tanzania's reluctance to agree to the IMF's lending terms (Havnevik *et al.*, 1988, p. 126).

Chapter 6

The Tanzanian Experience

Introduction

This chapter analyses the economic determinants of political stability in Tanzania since its independence in 1961 — a period that includes a peaceful democratic transition in 1994[1]. Although the analysis does not provide a full account of historical, political and economic developments, it addresses those aspects relevant to political stability throughout the period. It focuses particularly on the evolution of socio-economic and political structures and institutions.

Tanganyika became a German protectorate in 1885 and was administered by Germany until its defeat in the First World War, which led to the transfer of its administration to the UK under the League of Nations mandate in 1920. Both German and British colonial rule emphasised the production of cash crops and established plantations that used African labour. Compulsory agricultural production and distribution schemes that discriminated against Africans provoked a wide-based rural opposition that started in the early 1900s and grew into the national independence movement which gathered momentum in the 1950s. In 1946, Tanzania became a United Nations trust territory, which formally obliged the UK to prepare for its independence. The British administration, hoping it would lead to continuity of colonial economic policies, tried to create an African middle class by permitting African co-operatives[2] and by providing limited opportunities for Africans to engage in the state administration in the early 1950s.

The independence movement that had started with rural opposition to colonial practices strengthened under the leadership of the Tanganyika African National Union (TANU). TANU was formed in 1954 by Julius Nyerere — a teacher in a Roman Catholic school from 1945 — and with the support of the educated elite who organised themselves in African teachers' and civil service clubs. Co-operatives and the unions in the expanding urban sectors also increasingly organised to oppose growing inequalities. In the late 1950s, a series of strikes took place in protest against the discriminatory provision of social services and the inadequate representation of Africans in the civil service. The British attempted to weaken the independence movement by sponsoring a political party led by chiefs and expatriates — the United Tanganyika Party (UTP). The attempt failed. Consequently, the first general elections in 1957 saw a sweeping victory of the TANU and a peaceful transition to an African majority in the government.

Tanganyika obtained full independence in 1961 and the united republic named Tanzania came into existence in 1964, a year after Zanzibar became independent. Zanzibar has had a disproportionate influence on the union's economic and political affairs because the Arabs, who dominated the political and economic affairs of the island, also largely controlled Tanganyika's commerce during the colonial period[3]. Nyerere viewed union with the island as strategically important because of the Arabs' role in commerce and their potentially powerful position as a Muslim minority, especially in view of the high degree of political instability in neighbouring countries. Thus, while TANU and the Afro-Shirazi Party remained as the respective political parties of Tanganyika and Zanzibar, their leaders alternatively became the President and the Vice-President of the Union until 1977. The Afro-Shirazi Party merged with the TANU in that year, forming *Chama Cha Mapinduzi* (CCM — Revolutionary Party) as the single party of the Union-wide one-party system, with Nyerere as the President.

This chapter focuses primarily on the political economy of mainland Tanzania which has more than 95 per cent of the Union's population; it confines references to Zanzibar to those events and socio-economic and political characteristics of the island of relevance to analysis of Tanzania as a whole[4]. While production and distribution relations established by the German and British colonial regimes discriminated heavily against native Tanganyikans, the resulting lack of major socio-economic divisions among the Africans contributed significantly to African unity. The absence of ethnic-based segregation and the use of a common language, Swahili, were among the fundamental elements that helped to achieve a unified independence movement as well as post-independence political stability in Tanzania. The ideology of the post-independence government, moreover, aimed for equality, although it did so without carefully designed policies to achieve or sustain this objective. Throughout most of the post-independence period ideologist and pragmatic groups competed continuously within the state administration, the former dominating the state until the 1980s and the latter — which gave priority to growth and favoured a relatively liberal approach to development — gaining influence since then[5].

Education and health facilities saw substantial improvements from independence up to the mid-1970s, but Tanzania failed to generate sustainable growth and thus to maintain basic social services. After the mid-1970s, a series of exogenous shocks, and inefficiencies associated with a high degree of state intervention, resulted in a severe economic crisis. This led to signs of political conflict by the mid-1980s. The government responded with both accommodation and repression. In view of deteriorating capacity to achieve equality or growth by the 1980s, it gradually initiated economic reforms which accelerated in the second half of the 1980s under adjustment programmes supported by the international financial institutions. Since then signs of recovery and dynamism in the economy have slowly emerged.

76

In 1995, Tanzania made a peaceful transition to multiparty democracy as a result of both donor pressures and the CCM's attempt to accommodate growing domestic protests against corruption and civil rights abuses. Nonetheless, the first multiparty elections in 1995 left the Union government that had held power since 1964 virtually unchallenged, despite the emergence of about a dozen political parties. After the democratic transition, the main potential threat to political stability has taken the form of tension between the financially advantaged minority Asian and European groups and the native Tanzanians. The Union between Arab-dominated Zanzibar and mainland Tanzania has also continued to present a delicate and sometimes uneasy balance manifest in the recurrent theme of Zanzibar's sub-nationalism.

Fundamental Determinants of Political Stability

Despite the presence of many tribal groups, natives of Tanganyika enjoyed a non-segregated society due to a common language and the lack of any group with a dominating majority or social status. The absence of alternatives to subsistence farming and to wage labour on plantations for most of the colonial period also reinforced the homogeneity of the African population. Moreover, the colonial administrations did not create any significant social or occupational segregation among Africans. The independence movement was therefore unified and wide-based. Lack of divisions within African society, along with adherence to the ideology of equality in the post-independence period, has also contributed in important respects to political stability.

Lack of Major Socio-Economic Segregation Among the Africans

The absence of ethnic conflicts among Africans provides a very important element of political stability in Tanzania. Most native Africans have Bantu origins. While the population has been classified into about 120 tribal groups, no one group has a dominating position in the population. Moreover, tribes have historically lived in sparsely populated areas, chieftainship was not prevalent (chiefs were generally not very dominant or powerful) and there has been no significant tribal conflict or armed struggle. Thus on independence Tanzania inherited a relatively peaceful tradition.

The use of a common language, Swahili (or Kiswahili)[6], has also been a favourable element in uniting the Africans, whereas in many other colonies the use of a colonial language contributed to the separation of a local elite from the rest of African society. The diverse, yet not segregated, nature of Tanzania's ethnic composition facilitated unity in its independence movement as well as continuity in its post-independence administration. The lack of any significant associations between particular tribal groups and social or occupational categories contributed to this ethnic unity. Civil servants in large cities, for example, were recruited from various tribes. The post-independence government pursued deliberate policies to reinforce these features of national unity.

The colonial administrations of Germany (1885-1920) and the United Kingdom (1920-59) did not invest much in the manufacturing sector. Moreover, while the German colonial administration set up plantations that used African labour to extract revenues from cash crops, Africans were prohibited from cash-crop cultivation[7]. In the 1950s, freehold land extended to about two-thirds of the total area under cultivation. The Africans, however, were largely alienated from the land (Havnevik, 1993, p. 31). African enrolment in commerce was also discouraged or prevented; plantations and export-import companies were mostly owned by the Europeans, and the Asians dominated domestic trade and commerce.

The transfer of the colonial administration to the United Kingdom after the First World War reinforced both the existing economic structure and production relations. Other British colonies in East Africa, Kenya and Uganda in particular had more favourable positions than Tanganyika in industrial development. Although the British colonial administration implemented some elements of industrial policy geared to import substitution after the Second World War, industrial investment in Tanganyika remained negligible. The manufacturing sector, which produced import substitutes for consumption goods, was dominated by a few multinationals, which also controlled the financial and trade sectors. Africans were excluded from the middle and senior ranks in both government and the private sector, and surplus from import substitution was largely transferred abroad. At independence, agriculture generated about 60 per cent of Tanzanian output, while industry accounted for only about 3 to 4 per cent. Africans constituted the majority of agricultural producers (about 90 per cent of the whole population), workers and a small number of teachers and civil servants[8].

The colonial administration discriminated against Africans in favour of the well-connected Asian traders and European businesses. Although the education policy of 1947-56 provided primary education and middle school agricultural education for all racial groups, secondary education expanded only for the Europeans and Asians. In 1960, half of the education budget was spent on foreigners, about 2 per cent of the population; only 25 per cent of the Africans attended primary schools; and the adult literacy rate among the Africans was 10 per cent. Access to other social services was similarly unfavourable for Africans. These discriminatory colonial policies nonetheless constituted a unifying force in the African population.

Unified and Wide-based Support for the Independence Movement

The first major rebellion against colonial rule occurred under the Germans during 1905-06: the *Maji-Maji* rebellion, provoked by Africans' alienation from the land through taxation and the use of force to make them work on the plantations. The military suppression of the rebellion led to a major weakening of African traditional societies, which were to be further hit by the First World War, famines and diseases. Starting in the 1930s, the British administration used the Native Authorities to implement compulsory agricultural development schemes for the cultivation of export commodities and to impose monopoly marketing arrangements. The high degree of coercion and increased inequality that accompanied these policies led to severe rural unrest by the end of the 1940s. As the rural-based opposition to colonial rule strengthened, the position of the Native Authorities deteriorated. By the end of the 1940s, in reaction to the growing popular opposition, the colonial Governor imposed further restrictions on nationalist political activities.

In 1929, the African Association (AA) had formed to unite all Africans against colonial rule. AA grew out of the Tanganyika Territory African Civil Servants Association, formed in 1922 to unite the Christian and Muslim civil servants and renamed the Tanganyika African Association (TAA) in 1948, after Zanzibar was expelled for passing confidential information to the colonial authorities.

In the 1930s, the trade-union movement grew independently, led by a former leader of the African Welfare and Commercial Association, who objected to the elitism of AA. Opposition to colonial rule thus strengthened throughout the colonial period and became manifest in the riots and strikes by trade-union workers during 1937-39, a general strike joined by relatively more skilled workers in 1947, and a major riot that led to violence and a subsequent ban on the union movement in 1950.

During the 1950s, British colonial rule aimed to create an African middle class in order to generate African support for colonial policies and thus reinforce the colonial mode of production. To this end, in 1952, the colonial administration permitted African co-operatives to develop to replace the Asians in marketing African produce. Co-operative societies marketed an increasing proportion of the African crops. They had a membership of close to 20 per cent of farm families, mostly among the relatively wealthier ones[9]. While co-operatives led to regional imbalances and increased inequality among Africans, they also helped to demonstrate the ability of Africans to succeed in business. In 1955, the British administration permitted trade unions to reorganise and the Tanganyika Federation of Labour (TFL) formed to co-ordinate all unions under the leadership of the Tanzanian elite, in contrast to the 1930s and 1940s when unskilled labour led the unions.

The union movement strengthened. By the second half of the 1950s, large numbers of Africans had been organised in trade unions, co-operative societies and teachers' and civil servants' clubs[10]. In 1954, following Nyerere's appointment to lead the TAA, it converted into a political party and was renamed TANU. To promote national unity, TANU aimed to eliminate tribalism and any form of racialism. Although the TFL was organised independently from the political parties and not affiliated with TANU, it collaborated closely with TANU in the independence movement by mobilising the urban labour force and organising strikes. Leaders of trade and co-operative unions supported the independence movement, mobilising millions including the educated and illiterate, rural and urban, Muslims and Christians. Between 1954 and 1957, TANU's membership grew from 15 000 to 200 000.

The colonial administration's decision, under pressure from the Colonial Office and the UN, to encompass the Africans in the Legislative Council led to only disproportionately small African representation: of 43 Councillors, the colonial Governor appointed 21 — seven each for Europeans, Asians and Africans, although the population as a whole had 400 Africans for every European. This provoked further African opposition to the colonial administration. In 1957, British colonial rule attempted to assert its power further by replacing the Native Authority Councils with all-African District Councils, but these had to report to multiracial Provincial Councils. This reorganisation aimed to secure control over local governments by the European and Asian majority in the government. It too resulted in increased public support for TANU in the independence struggle. The colonial administration also sponsored chiefs and white settlers in forming a rival party in 1956, the United Tanganyika Party (UTP), to weaken the opposition.

In addition to the colonial administration's efforts to suppress the independence movement, a split from the TANU's leadership in 1958 led to the formation of the Tanganyika African National Congress (TANC), challenging both the political power of TANU and its ideology of unity and equality. TANC represented Africans only. Like the UTP, however, it was completely outvoted in the elections of 1958 and 1960. This proved African unity against the colonial rule far stronger than the special interests of the middle-class Africans that the colonial administration attempted to create to support itself. Full independence came in 1961 after a sweeping victory of TANU, which gained an impressive number of rural supporters in the first general elections in 1960.

Post-independence Determinants of Political Stability

During the colonial period, infrastructure had developed mainly to support export-oriented production, especially sisal, cotton and coffee in the Central and Northern regions. This laid the foundations of uneven regional development. Nonetheless, the post-independence government's effective grass-roots organisation and provision of social services to the larger population secured wide-based political support and permitted a reasonably stable political environment.

Government policies that aimed for equality also helped to prevent the emergence of political opposition groups. Such policies included the use of Swahili as the official language rather than English which was spoken by only a small elite; the villagisation schemes that led to the relocation of the majority of the population and thus may have weakened tribal connections — not the intended goal; and boarding schools for secondary education in regions far away from home which may also have helped weaken tribal connections. Furthermore, the government expanded its economic and political control by nationalisation, the creation of parastatals and the extension of the power of central government at local levels.

Periods of post-independence political conflict, manifested mainly in the form of strikes, posed no serious threat to political stability. In the early 1960s, political conflict arose from the unsatisfied demands of those more organised and actively involved in the independence movement — mainly the trade unionists — who had expected to take over the privileges enjoyed by the former administrators. In the early 1970s and 1980s, however, political conflict arose mainly in reaction to abuses by the local authorities and growing inequality.

The government's response took the forms of both accommodating demands, by improving socio-economic status through redistributive policies, and suppressing elements of civil society. The accommodative response included the establishment of legal mechanisms to prevent abuses of power. The government, however, also limited the emergence of political alternatives or special interests by reducing or eliminating the autonomy of civil-society organisations. For instance, during the 1970s, it restricted the union movement and made it subordinate to government; eliminated independent village associations; and formed the TANU Youth League, which also acted as a militia. Given the peaceful tradition of the society and achievements with regard to equal provision of social services, the repressive policies did not aggravate political opposition substantially.

Within the state apparatus, a major split emerged between ideological and pragmatic socialists, the former giving priority to equality, the latter to growth-oriented development policies. Since independence, the evolution of institutions and economic policies has often reflected the struggle between these two groups. Although pragmatic socialists did not question socialist ideology and its objective of equality, they advocated more liberal economic policies and thus differed from ideological socialists with regard to the means to achieve a socialist construction. In the 1970s, ideological socialists, who dominated the party, also increased their control over the state. By the 1980s, however, their policies failed to achieve the long-term growth and sustainable resource mobilisation needed to maintain good social services. Consequently a transition followed towards more liberal economic policies in the 1980s, as pragmatic socialists began to dominate the government.

Legal and Institutional Measures of Political Stability

TANU led the independence movement with widely based rural and urban support. Its maintenance of an effective grass-roots organisation and its emphasis on equality enabled it to remain the majority party with no major political alternative even after transition to a multiparty system in 1994. The use of Swahili, along with English, as the official language and the provision of primary school and health facilities for almost all the population were among the crucial elements of national unity and equality. In addition, the government initiated legal and constitutional changes to consolidate its political authority.

After independence, Nyerere resigned as Prime Minister and was replaced by Rashidi Kawawa, founder of the Tanganyika Federation of Labour (TFL). In 1962, Tanganyika became a Republic with Nyerere as President. Kawawa replaced the Native Authorities with locally elected District Councils. In 1964, Tanganyika became a one-party state and Nyerere was re-elected as President. The one-party state had a democratic element that allowed two candidates, nominated by District Conferences subject to the approval of the National Executive Committee, to contest each seat. Many local candidates won the 1965 elections against the incumbents (Hyden, 1986, p. 56). To reinforce national unity, the electoral law of 1965 prohibited promotion of racial and regional divisions (Hyden, 1986, p. 43).

In the immediate aftermath of independence, trade unions that had closely collaborated with TANU during the independence movement generated the main political conflicts. Their leaders, who replaced Kawawa and several other moderates chosen as cabinet ministers, organised strikes for wage increases. In reaction, a series of Acts in 1962 restricted strike action, prohibited civil servants from joining trade unions and increased the authority of the TFL over other unions. In 1964, the National Union of Tanganyika (NUTA) replaced the TFL in order to unify the union movement and subordinate it to TANU.

Besides increasing control over trade unionism, however, the government also accommodated the demands of workers by raising minimum wages, doubling average wage earnings between 1960 and 1963. Although attempts to replace expatriates in the civil service with equally qualified Africans were made, Nyerere opposed excessive Africanisation[11]. In 1964, an army mutiny occurred over dissatisfaction with wages and the slow progress in replacing high-ranking British army officers. After it was contained with the help of the British army, the army was rebuilt excluding the British officers.

In 1967, the Arusha Declaration laid out Nyerere's vision of Tanzanian socialism, emphasising public ownership, education for self-reliance, the importance of agriculture over industry and rural over urban development. In 1971, to prevent government officials from engaging in rent-seeking activities, TANU Guidelines prohibited party officials from holding any shares or offices in companies and any rent-earning properties[12]. The Guidelines also permitted increased state control over production and distribution to achieve the objective of socialism for self-reliance. TANU consolidated its control over the economy through nationalisation in various sectors; a form of decentralisation of government, which amounted to increased powers of the central government at the local level; and accelerating the process of villagisation to organise production and distribution according to the socialist objectives that emphasised equitable provision of education and health. The TANU Youth League, established as a mechanism of social control, helped the government in its villagisation process in the early 1970s. The *Newspaper Act* and the *Tanzania News Agency Act* of 1976 also enhanced the state's control over civil society.

To accommodate the workers following socialist ideology, Workers' Committees were established in 1964 with members elected at the enterprise level. Workers' Councils were established in 1970 for worker participation in management. In 1969, a constitutional amendment permitted TANU to establish party branches in industries. From 1971 to 1973, workers who did not co-operate with the NUTA and who protested abuses by parastatal management staged a series of strikes and factory seizures. The government intervened and many lost their jobs. The state explained this suppression by saying that industrial workers were already better paid than the majority of the population and that granting them additional privileges was not justified (McHenry, 1994, p. 134).

Decentralisation of the government administration aimed to consolidate government and party power at local levels. A notable example involved the 1969 dissolution of the Ravuma Development Association (RAD), founded by Nyerere in 1960 as an independent organisation to run *ujamaa* villages[13]. In 1969, RAD comprised 17 villages and had emerged as an independent administrative organ. It operated as an efficient institution for the organisation of production and marketing and provided basic social services, such as education and health, to its villagers (von Freyhold, 1979, p. 75). In 1972, Area and Regional Commissioners appointed by the central government replaced the locally elected and self-reliant District Councils in order to restrict local political activity and eliminate the potential for independent local political mobilisation. Decentralisation of the government administration to the local level also helped TANU to maintain its political support by confining complaints about local problems, as well as their resolution, to local administration. It also aimed to bring planning and implementation to the regional and district levels (Hyden, 1986, p. 59).

Due to their respective emphases on ideology and pragmatism, the party and government provided checks on each other. For example, members of the Parliament often drew attention to local abuses by the Regional and Area Commissioners, which led to the institutionalisation of a control mechanism over the bureaucratic class through the establishment of a Permanent Commission of Inquiry (Hyden, 1986, p. 46). In 1982, Area and Regional Commissioners were separated from the District and Regional Party Secretaries to eliminate abuse of power by the commissioners. In 1984, after the central government failed to provide basic social services in the face of the economic crisis of the second half of the 1970s, District Councils were re-introduced. Although they received authority to collect local taxes for local purposes, they nonetheless failed to reverse the trend of deteriorating economic performance and increased corruption.

Dissolution of Co-operative Unions in 1976 provided another example of increased state authority. Co-operatives were generally seen to exacerbate inequality given that they facilitated the development of profitable agricultural activities that mostly favoured better-off farmers. By dissolving them, the government intended to promote a better distribution of public goods while increasing its control over economic activity. Consequently, Crop Authorities took over the roles of marketing, extension, crop processing and transportation. They proved highly inefficient, however, and co-operatives were re-instituted in 1982. In the 1980s, some financial incentives were restored for private farmers, including village smallholders, although peasants who had been relocated in the villagisation movement were not permitted to move back.

Meanwhile, constitutional changes included an amendment in 1975 that officially marked the principles of socialism and self-reliance. A Union-wide, one-party constitution in 1977 led to the merger of the Afro-Shirazi Party of Zanzibar with TANU under *Chama Cha Mapinduzi* (CCM — Revolutionary Party). The Union constitution mitigated to some extent the potential threats that the recurrent theme of Zanzibari subnationalism has posed for Tanzania's political stability. It also benefited Zanzibar in a deteriorating economic situation aggravated by a decline in the price of cloves, Zanzibar's main income-generating product. CCM guidelines reinforced the commitment to the socialist ideology. CCM maintained its monopoly party position until the constitutional amendment in 1992 that led to a multiparty system. It nonetheless has continued as the single most popular party.

Socio-economic Determinants of Political Stability

TANU's main objectives were the equitable distribution of wealth and African advancement. Major tools of the government to achieve equality included incomes policies and public provision of education and health services. Until 1967, no major policy changes occurred and the private sector was not discouraged. A watershed came in 1967 when "socialism for self-reliance" became the slogan of development strategy, as defined in the Arusha Declaration. This was partly a response to the government's failure to mobilise as much foreign aid as it had predicted.

Following the Arusha Declaration, the state acquired major means of production through nationalisation of a significant part of the industry, finance and trade sectors. With the *ujamaa* villagisation schemes in the 1970s, the government aimed to reinforce its control over production and distribution. Slow progress in voluntary villagisation in the early 1970s, however, led the government to launch a major effort in 1973 to relocate rural population to *ujamaa* villages, involving the armed forces[14]. The villagisation process often destroyed the former dwellings of relocated farmers. In 1973, only 13 per cent of the population had relocated voluntarily, but by 1976, 85 per cent of the population had been relocated to 8 000 *ujamaa* villages. To accommodate the newly established villages and reinforce rural development, more than 40 per cent of development spending went to infrastructure between 1971 and 1974 (Stewart, 1986, p. 49).

Although the Arusha Declaration did not rule out private business, it aimed to increase state control over the organisation of production and to facilitate a more equitable distribution of wealth across the nation. Consequently, it nationalised all commercial banks, the grain milling industry, the largest foreign-owned import-export houses, and controlling shares in the subsidiaries of multinational companies in the late 1960s[15]. It also established many parastatals, whose numbers rose from 47 in 1967 to 139 by 1974 and reached 425 in 1984 (Moshi, 1992)[16]. By 1974, the state owned between 80 per cent and 85 per cent of all medium to large firms (McHenry, 1994, p. 131). The public sector's share in manufacturing thus rose from 14 per cent in 1967 to 57 per cent in 1982 and in manufacturing employment from 15.5 per cent to 53 per cent. By the early 1970s, 90 per cent of new capital formation came from the state (World Bank, 1975).

Probably the most important reason for the wide-based political support of the post-independence government was the progress it achieved in providing basic education and health services. To improve the social status of the population at large, it directed resource allocation here rather than to the creation of a small and highly educated class of technocrats. It established very successful universal primary education and adult education programmes and opened health centres throughout the country rather than large hospitals accessible only by a few. During 1971-74, education was the single largest item (16 per cent) in total government spending (Stewart, 1986, p. 49). As a result, literacy increased from 10 per cent in 1960 to 30 per cent in 1970 and 70 per cent by the end of the 1970s. Life expectancy rose and child mortality fell substantially. As of 1993, health indicators compared very favourably with the rest of sub-Saharan Africa[17].

Table 6.1. **Social Indicators in Tanzania, 1970-90**

	1970	1975	1980	1985	1990
Primary School					
Gross Enrolment Rate (per cent of age group)	32	34	53	93	75
Secondary School					
Gross Enrolment Rate (per cent of age group)	2	3	3	3	3
Life Expectancy at Birth (years)			45		51
Infant Mortality (per thousand live births)		132	125	119	98
Access to Safe Water (per cent of population)					
Rural		9	36		42
Urban		6	88		88

Source: World Bank (1995*b*).

The government also tried to eliminate inequalities by compressing wage differentials, both reducing the top salaries and increasing the minimum wage. With the increased role of the state in the 1970s, the number of civil servants increased by 11 per cent per year on average (Galli, ed., 1981, p. 153). Despite progressive taxation, civil servants enjoyed relatively high incomes due to both tax evasion and fringe benefits. Eighty per cent of the regional budget went to salaries of public workers (Galli, ed., 1981, p. 141). Although rural-urban wage inequalities did not fall, urban wage differentials did, substantially. In 1961, the ratio of the highest civil service wage to the lowest was 50:1; it dropped to 9:1 by 1974 and to 6:1 by 1981.

To summarise, post-independence political stability in Tanzania arose largely from the state's benevolence in providing social services to achieve socio-economic equality. Socialist development policies, coupled with socio-economic characteristics conducive to political stability, generated a large measure of political support. The state's ability to maintain this support despite the lack of well-designed economic policies and growing economic hardship, however, came also from large amounts of foreign aid, especially during the 1970s.

The state became increasingly more authoritarian — in its control over both the civil service and the economy — to counteract slow progress in implementing its developmental policies. It thus attempted to centralise the organisation of production and distribution by means of the villagisation programmes and nationalising major means of production. It increased its control over civil society to maintain a political consensus and to reinforce the effectiveness of policy implementation.

Increased state intervention in the economy and the extension of central government control to local levels, in turn, created opportunities for rent-seeking by bureaucrats and local civil servants. Budgetary balances deteriorated as decentralisation of the government in 1972 implied both decentralisation of spending decisions and centralisation of revenue collection, leading local governments to demand greater amounts of resources from the central government. Centralised pricing and marketing policies reduced incentives for productive activities and increased inefficiencies and inequalities. Economic decline started in the late 1970s, due partly to a series of shocks, including the war with Uganda and worsening terms of trade; but it came also from inappropriate macroeconomic policies and ill-designed development policies whose effects the adverse shocks partly masked. The large amounts of foreign aid in the 1970s from those sympathetic to Tanzania's genuine effort to achieve equality probably also led to the postponement of popular pressure for economic and institutional reforms until the 1980s.

The analysis of the post-independence political economy of Tanzania suggests that political stability, although perhaps necessary, does not suffice for growth. Political stability in Tanzania in fact permitted the perpetuation of bad economic policies which in turn aggravated the ensuing economic hardship. One can argue that the firm stand of the post-independence government on the equality-growth trade-off (in favour of the former) and a general lack of human capacity limited policy choices and their chances of success.

Failure to Take Off and the Transition to Multiparty Democracy

The post-independence government succeeded in improving the basic education and health status of the people significantly, especially by the end of the 1970s. Nevertheless, it failed to achieve sustainable economic growth; from the late 1960s, managerial and bureaucratic abuses and repressed incentives for productive activities rendered the economy highly inefficient[18]. This, coupled with the effects of unfavourable shocks throughout the 1970s, reduced the state's capacity to provide basic social services. Increased unemployment and repressed private entrepreneurship led to growing opposition to prevailing policies while strengthening the position of pragmatists in the state. The CCM's initial response to the rising opposition was one of suppression, although by the mid-1980s it conceded that the lack of resources needed to revitalise the economy and to maintain a socialist structure made economic reforms inevitable. Consequently, the CCM progressively launched economic reforms during the 1980s. Up to the mid-1980s, however, these attempts remained limited in scope and optimistic in assumptions, and failed to achieve much success. As a result, pragmatists increasingly started to dominate the state. The transition to a multiparty system in 1995 resulted from mounting domestic and international pressures which identified economic failures with the political regime.

Economic Downturn

Increased inefficiencies in parastatals and local administrations, droughts between 1973 and 1975, the oil crises of 1974 and 1978, declining terms of trade, the breakdown of the East African community in 1977 and the Uganda war between 1977 and 1979 — all contributed to the substantial economic decline that became particularly evident in the second half of the 1970s. While average per capita GDP grew by more than 3 per cent during 1961-67 and by 1.5 per cent during 1968-75, it declined on average by 1.5 per cent between 1976 and 1985, falling by the mid-1980s to a level even lower than in 1966. Meanwhile, industrial production fell by 11.3 per cent between 1980 and 1985 — against a cumulative doubling during 1967-77 — as industrial capacity use fell to about 20 per cent. Starting from the late 1970s, the budget deficit also deteriorated substantially, reaching around 9 per cent of GDP in the 1980s, up from about 4 per cent in the late 1960s. Table 6.2 provides the main macroeconomic indicators for four sub-periods after independence; it shows that while economic performance in the 1970s was worse than in the late 1960s, crises did not become evident until the 1980s. A relative recovery in terms of output growth and fiscal balances occurred starting from 1987. Figure 6.1 traces the development of fiscal imbalances from 1966 to 1995.

Table 6.2. **Evolution of Macroeconomic Indicators in Tanzania**

Period	GDP	GDP per Capita	(Consumer Price Index change) Inflation	Domestic Saving	Fiscal Deficit
	(Rate of change at 1987 prices)		(Per cent per year)	(Percentages of GDP)	
1967-69	5.97	1.02	13.49	17.31	4.29
1970-79	3.95	0.58	10.99	14.17	6.72
1980-86	1.41	-1.67	30.53	10.28	10.09
1987-95	4.16	1.02	28.97	6.39	6.18

Source: World Bank data (1997, various, World Development Indicators CD-ROM).

87

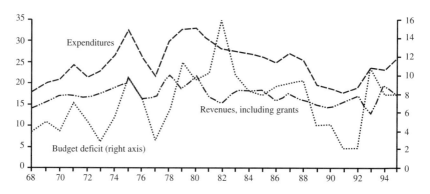

Figure 6.1. **Fiscal Balances: 1966-95**
(in percentage of GDP)

Throughout the 1970s, the resource balance remained negative as the share of exports in GDP fell from about 25 per cent in 1970 to less than 10 per cent in the early 1980s. In 1975, foreign reserves became almost exhausted and they remained negligible throughout the 1980s. Real imports also fell, on average by 1.5 per cent per year during the 1970s and by more than 20 per cent between 1982 and 1983. While the trade balance worsened during the 1970s (except in 1976-77 during a coffee price boom), the government managed to maintain a roughly constant level of investment by relying on increased foreign aid. Figure 6.2 shows the deteriorating trend of the current account balance.

Figure 6.2. **Current Account Balance: 1966-95**
GDP shares, current prices

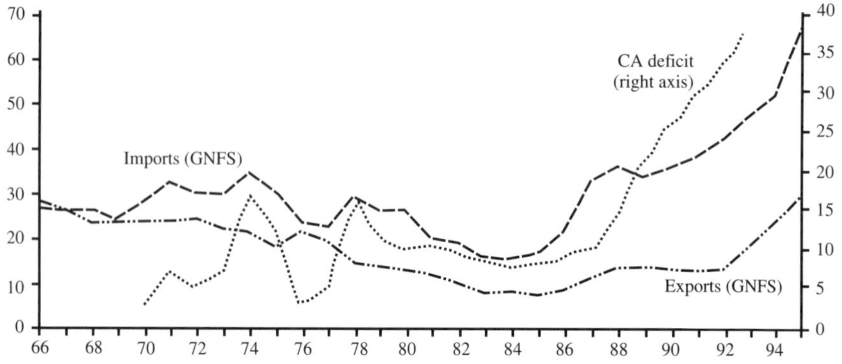

Foreign aid more than quadrupled as a percentage of imports between 1970 and 1985 and almost doubled as a percentage of trade deficits between 1970 and 1980. The share of capital goods imports rose from 31 per cent in 1971 to 54 per cent in

1986. Foreign-aid dependency made the economic crisis even more severe, especially as the terms of lending to Tanzania worsened substantially in the early 1980s. Net loans declined by more than 60 per cent, short-term debt doubled and total grants roughly halved between 1980 and 1985. When Tanzania finalised an agreement with the IMF for the adoption of the Economic Reform Programme in 1986, more than half of the short-term debt was converted to long-term concessional loans, mitigating the short-term balance of payments problems (Havnevik *et al.*, 1988, p. 122). As Figure 6.3 demonstrates, increased foreign aid since the mid-1980s did not lead to a sustained increase in domestic savings, although it did produce an increased share of investment in GDP.

Figure 6.3. **Savings, Investment and Per Capita GDP Trends**

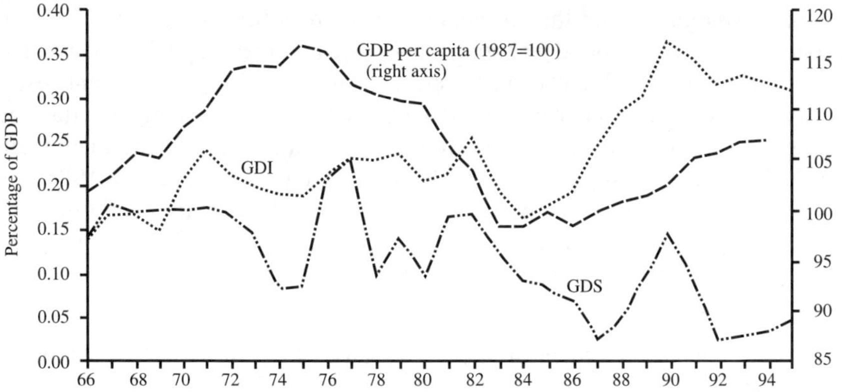

Note: GDI = gross domestic investment; GDS = gross domestic savings.

Institutional Failures

Notwithstanding substantial improvements of social services in the 1960s and early 1970s, a combination of unfavourable exogenous shocks and inappropriate economic policies led to a severe economic downturn by the 1980s. The inappropriate economic policies included an overvalued exchange rate, extensive state controls over marketing and production, a substantially increased number of inefficient parastatals, and reduced incentives to the private sector. In addition, the main instrument for facilitating the provision of education and health services, the *ujamaa* policies, caused a major resource drain from the costs of relocating a large segment of the population and difficulties in efficiently managing central resource allocation. The villagisation process also generated land pressure through over-cultivation and deforestation. Rapid population growth, despite the accompanying rapid urbanisation, contributed to this trend.

The extension of central government powers, accompanied by the dissolution of co-operatives, did not have equitable results. For instance, Tanganyika Rural Development Bank (TRDB) provided only 11 per cent to 17 per cent of its funds to *ujamaa* villages between 1971 and 1973, while the rest went to established co-operatives, parastatals and a few better-off individual farmers. In 1973, only 1.4 per cent of the registered villages were aided and 60 per cent of the TRDB's credits went to tobacco and tea, of which 97.5 per cent went to only three out of 20 regions/*ujamaa* villages (Galli, ed., 1981, p. 152). Price controls on essential goods, intended to benefit the poor whose spending was largely on such essentials, furnished another mechanism of state interference. This policy failed to serve its purpose as parallel markets developed; the well-connected apparently became the major beneficiaries of controlled prices. Price controls also greatly distorted the incentive structure for agricultural production.

The government had established parastatals to achieve import substitution through industrial development and thus to generate resources for domestic investment, but these parastatals used imported technology and were relatively capital-intensive, leading to increased import dependence. Their share of manufacturing investment rose from 12 per cent in 1966 to 63 per cent in 1970. Acute foreign exchange shortage led to rationing of foreign exchange among industries. Value added in the manufacturing sector declined from 12.4 per cent of GDP in 1972 to 6 or 7 per cent in 1986; despite inefficiencies and lack of foreign exchange for essential inputs the sector nonetheless maintained profits because real industrial wages declined by about 70 per cent (Havnevik *et al.*, 1988, p. 147)[19]. In addition, parastatals created opportunities for abuses by middle- and high-ranking Africans.

Although the government did not target large-scale farming, nationalisation of the estates and some *ujamaa* settlements had this very effect; in 1980, 80 per cent of development expenditure went to large-scale farming (Stewart, 1986, p. 50). The monopoly position of parastatals both in the manufacturing sector and in agricultural marketing also hurt smallholder agricultural development in the 1970s, particularly because major finance institutions were nationalised and diverted their funds mainly towards the parastatals. Between 1975 and 1981, food crops received the highest share (46 per cent) of agricultural development spending, of which parastatal sugar development by itself took 71 per cent. Of the livestock development budget, 78 per cent went to the parastatals sector, which accounts for only 2 per cent of the national herd (Havnevik *et al.*, 1988, p. 36). In 1986, parastatals got 73 per cent of Tanzania Investment Bank loans, 54 per cent of which were in arrears (as were 65 per cent of the TRDB loans in 1980; Stewart, 1986, p. 58). Likewise, 65 per cent of the loan portfolio of the National Bank of Commerce went to parastatals because the foreign exchange allocation system also favoured them. As a result of the lack of sufficient incentives in productive sectors, the shares of agriculture and manufacturing in GDP fell, while those of commerce, finance and public administration rose between 1966 and 1985 (World Bank, 1990*b*, p. 82).

Failure to Attain Developmental Objectives

In the 1970s, the government's policy of education for self-reliance emphasised primary education with a focus on improving agricultural production. Private secondary education began to emerge, especially in relatively better-off regions where primary and secondary education facilities were more developed. By the 1980s, economic downturn deprived the government of funds needed to maintain its previous level of education spending. The share of education in total government spending declined from 17 per cent in 1974 to 7 per cent in 1985, while that of health fell from 9 per cent to 5 per cent over the same period. Between 1983 and 1991, the literacy rate dropped by 7 per cent among the poor but increased among the better-off; while 6 per cent of the better-off had been to secondary school, only 1 per cent of the poor had this advantage. Of the 20 regions in the early 1990s, in only two, Arusha and Klimanjaro, did more than 10 per cent of the population above school age have secondary or higher education.

Hence, the government's objective of eliminating regional biases had become severely constrained by the 1980s. Although more than one-third of total secondary education was private by 1984, the increase in such facilities could not compensate for the decline in public spending: despite an increase in absolute numbers, the secondary school enrolment rate fell from 29.2 per cent in 1963 to 6.4 per cent in 1986. The District Councils reintroduced in 1984 and allowed to collect local taxes to fund the recurrent costs of primary education and health services failed to fill these basic needs due to lack of resources and extensive corruption. As a result, access to education became a major factor distinguishing the poor and the better-off.

Incomes policies also failed to reduce rural-urban inequalities, although urban wage inequality improved slightly due to progressive wage reductions and taxation. According to Collier, however, rural income distribution worsened between 1969 and 1975 (Coulson, 1982, p. 7). In contrast, ILO (1982) reports that rural income distribution (excluding subsistence) improved over the same period. ILO also indicates that improved rural-urban income distribution arose mainly from the reduced incomes of the urban wage earners (Stewart, 1986, p. 30). Nevertheless, rural producers, urban workers, and upper income earners all fared worse at the end of the 1970s than at the beginning of the decade.

Economic Reforms and the Political Transition

As Table 6.2 above shows, Tanzania experienced relatively good economic performance with slight increases in average real per capita GDP until the end of 1970s. Although economic downturn began at the end of the 1960s, the impact did not become fully manifest until the 1980s. Nevertheless, in the face of increased economic difficulties from the mid-1970s, finance for the provision of health and education became scarce and abuses by parastatal managers and bureaucrats increased. Furthermore, foreign lending declined severely by the early 1980s.

In response to increasing protests of workers and businessmen against the worsening economic conditions, the *Economic Sabotage Act of 1983* gave extensive powers to the police to control overpricing and hoarding. The *Human Resources Deployment Act* increased state powers to contain threats to political instability; it led to civil rights violations, especially against the unemployed and the commercial middle class, often exempting high-ranking government officials. The campaign against "economic sabotage" led to mass arrests (1 139 persons, of whom 1 072 were businessmen; Havnevik, 1993, p. 59). In 1986, a field force unit killed a number of workers protesting about their wages in a sugar factory in Kilimanjaro.

Although the donor community as well as the public stayed generally silent about increasing repression in the 1970s, such incidents led to mounting popular pressure and a loss of legitimacy of the party, while the power of the commercial middle class grew. These developments — and especially an acute foreign exchange crisis — led the government to initiate a series of economic reform programmes. The reforms were gradual. In 1981, Tanzania launched its own National Economic Survival Programme (NESP), but it failed to mobilise sufficient resources for economic recovery. In 1984, a new structural adjustment programme supported by the World Bank included significant devaluation of the exchange rate and substantial increases in agricultural prices in addition to major reductions in subsidies.

Foreign aid increased from 1986, especially following an Economic Recovery Programme financed by the IMF and involving major marketing reforms, liberalisation of a substantial portion of prices by 1989, and a depreciation of the real exchange rate by 50 per cent between 1985 and 1990. The supply response of the agricultural sector to the increased private incentives led to near self-sufficiency in food by 1990. In the 1990s, market reforms intensified with the liberalisation of foreign exchange allocations and parastatal reforms.

The increased influence of the pragmatic faction in the state and rising pressures for substantial market reforms were factors behind Nyerere's resignation as President in 1985. Continuing as chairman of the CCM, he worked to reconstruct the link between the party and the people and to demobilise public support for the ideologist approach to development, although without as much success as in the 1960s. Ali Hassan Mwinyi[20], who replaced Nyerere as President, represented the pragmatists and implemented more substantial economic reforms that gained IMF support. He undertook a major cabinet reshuffle in reaction to public protests against increased corruption. He was unopposed and re-elected in the 1990 general elections.

The government's suppression of civil society abated in the late 1980s. It allowed independent non-daily newspapers in 1988; permitted a limited public platform of debate on human rights violations in 1991; and, with a new *Co-operative Act*, reduced

CCM's supervision over the co-operatives in the same year. The labour and co-operative unions, followed by many other civil organisations that had been subordinate to the party, gradually received autonomy after 1990.

By the end of 1980s, donors largely initiated the debate on multiparty politics. Recognising the weakening links between the party and the people in the 1980s and the inability of the party to serve them as it had in the early years of independence, Nyerere declared his support for the transition to a multiparty system to promote democracy. Meanwhile, several opposition parties had formed in Britain; in 1990, exile opposition groups formed the Tanzania Democratic Forum and Tanzania Youth Democratic Movement. In 1991, the leaders of the Tanzania Legal Education Trust Fund formed the Union for Multi-party Democracy and the Civic United Front (CUF).

In 1991, a Presidential Commission, composed of an equal number of Arabs and Africans from the CCM cabinet and with mixed views on the transition to a multiparty system, conducted a popular survey (of about 36 000 people). They recorded 77 per cent support for the existing one-party system. Under external pressure, CCM legalised the registration of opposition parties in 1992. Despite the emergence of many political parties, CCM still won a series of by-elections. Their legitimacy was widely disputed, however, because of the CCM's privileged access to the media, irregularities and registration problems which led to boycotts by the opposition parties. Amid signs of growing divisions along regional, religious and ethnic lines, the CCM retained its political power with 62 per cent of the votes in the 1995 elections — the first multiparty general elections since independence.

Although the fairness of the Zanzibari elections was open to question, the union elections were generally interpreted as reflecting the public's preference for Benjamin Mkapa, who replaced Mwinyi as President. Nyerere and the ideological socialists supported Mkapa, but he was also committed to implementing market reforms. Mwinyi's defeat came partly from the association of his term of presidency (1985-95) with increased corruption and managerial deficiencies and partly because his term coincided with significant turmoil from increased domestic and international pressures for economic reforms and political transition.

Prospects for Political Stability

Recent Economic Trends

From independence, Tanzania remained committed to equality among households and regions and this contributed to a large measure of political stability. The provision of basic education to everyone until the mid-1970s played an important role. Nevertheless, declining economic trends led to a reduction in the primary school enrolment rate, while secondary school enrolment remained very low. Since the 1980s, the emerging private secondary schools have accommodated the relatively better-off, but these schools will probably increase differences in socio-economic status among Africans. Although an increase in secondary education and skilled labour may contribute to economic growth and thus generate domestic resources for redistribution, the current severe decline in the government's financial and institutional ability to provide social services probably means that state action will not offset growing inequalities.

Corruption, too, has become a serious problem in Tanzania, notwithstanding various attempts to eliminate it through institutional and economic reforms. Major market reforms regarding price liberalisation, marketing and parastatal restructuring were launched in the late 1980s and early 1990s. The early 1990s also saw progress on privatisation of the banking and parastatal sectors. The main commercial bank that had controlled almost all of the banking sector accounted for about two-thirds of it in 1995; although this share is still high, private banks began to emerge in urban areas from 1993. Of 300 loss-making parastatals, 75 were sold by the end of 1995 and sales have continued since then. Workers have not opposed them, partly because the *Public Corporations Act of 1997* provided for the sale of 40 per cent of the shares to them at minimum cost (McHenry, 1994, p. 152).

The economy showed signs of recovery after the more substantial market reforms began in the mid-1980s. The population below the poverty line declined from 65 per cent to 51 per cent between 1983 and 1991. Although the incidence of rural poverty increased slightly between 1993 and 1995, land reform policies may ameliorate the situation (World Bank, 1996c, p. 65). As Figure 6.3 indicated, economic reforms from the mid-1980s brought slow but persistent recovery in the trend of per capita GDP, which recovered its 1970 level only by 1990, however. During 1986-95, the agricultural sector grew by 5.3 per cent a year, up from less than 3 per cent during 1975-85. Agricultural growth in Tanzania reached double the African average in the 1990s. Although the declining trend of agricultural exports reversed, agricultural exports remained lower than in the 1960s and 1970s.

Improvements in the agricultural sector also helped reduce poverty and stimulate other sectors of the economy. Real manufacturing output grew by about 4 per cent a year between 1987 and 1995, reversing its 1981-86 downtrend of about 5 per cent annually. Manufacturing capacity use rose to about 50 per cent. Improved access to foreign exchange and removal of price distortions largely contributed to these developments. Investment climbed to more than 10 per cent of GDP between 1985 and 1990. Although it retreated slightly thereafter, the investment/GDP ratio remained higher than in the previous decade.

Notwithstanding improvements in output growth, fiscal balances deteriorated during 1992-95. Foreign-aid dependency in the government budget remained a significant problem. Inflation was about 30 per cent in 1995, the average since 1980 although it had dropped to 20 per cent in 1992. According to the World Bank definitions, Tanzania's debt is well above sustainable levels in terms of both solvency (debt to GDP ratio) and liquidity (debt service to exports ratio) (Figure 6.4). Nonetheless, rapid progress on market reforms and high potential for economic growth from considerable unused land and capacity in manufacturing, mining and tourism, appear to offer considerable potential for economic improvement. If a dynamic market economy emerges it may increase inequality, initially at least, but a growing economy could provide the government with increased resources for social services, infrastructure and other forms of redistribution, thus helping to secure continued support for the market reforms and, in turn, contributing to political stability.

Figure 6.4. **Foreign Debt Indicators**

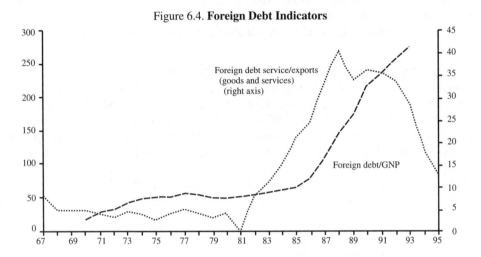

Political Trends

The constitutional amendment that legalised the multiparty system in 1992 prohibited tribal, religious and racial biases, to protect national unity. The pattern of politics after the multiparty constitution, however, has not differed much from those of other countries in the region undergoing a democratic transition. Several political parties formed along regional and ethnic lines, given the lack of major differences in economic policy agendas. For example, in 1995, a former member of the CCM cabinet formed the Convention for Construction and Reform (NCCR) that gathered support in the Kilimanjaro region. NCCR later joined a Zanzibari-dominated opposition group, the Civic United Front, that aimed for secession of Zanzibar, to contest the presidential elections in November 1995. The United Democratic Party (UDF) enjoys support among the largest ethnic group of Tanzania, the Sukuma. Political divisions, however, also often reflect personal rivalries and efforts to gain political power. When the former Minister of Finance had to resign in the face of allegations of financial wrongdoing, for example, he subsequently formed the National Reconstruction Alliance (NRA). With political divisions of such a personal nature, no significant political challenge to the CCM has thus far emerged.

The debates about sub-nationalism in both Zanzibar and the mainland present the greatest source of potential political division. As the national discussions for a transition to a multiparty democracy evolved from the late 1980s, discussions about Zanzibar's separation from the Union also intensified. The Arabs constitute the largest homogeneous ethnic and religious minority in the Union; they have dominated the economy and the politics of the island as well as commerce on the mainland. Although not self-sufficient, Zanzibar is a small island with good potential for growth based on the tourism and service sectors. This economic potential and the political incentives within a multiparty environment created a political trend in Zanzibar which favoured a split from the Union. Zanzibar's financial burden led some political groups in the mainland to favour a split as well.

In 1993, Zanzibar violated the 1964 Article of the Union and the 1977 Union Constitution by joining the Organisation of the Islamic Conference (OIC). This unconstitutional move led to cabinet reshuffles and, later, the withdrawal of Zanzibar from the OIC. It left Zanzibar's relationship with the mainland damaged. In 1993, the National Assembly unanimously passed legislation to form a third level of government — in addition to that of the mainland and the Union — to administer Zanzibar separately from the mainland. Nyerere criticised this decision severely because it violated the CCM's commitment to unity. The Parliament reversed it in 1994, but Zanzibar's split from the Union remains a major source of potential political division.

Asian traders and Europeans appear to be the main source of segregation in Tanzania, rather than ethnic and occupational distinctions among the indigenous Africans. Asians, especially, dominate profitable economic activities. Because most Africans do not have the means to acquire ownership or start a business, privatisation and market reforms are most likely to benefit the Asians and Europeans. This overlap of ethnicity, religion and occupation constitutes the greatest source of unrest among the mainland population; the unregistered Democratic Party, for instance, pursues political propaganda against the Asian traders and has provoked several attacks against them, which in turn led to counter-attacks. Although increased ethnic and occupational confrontations probably will spur tensions between the ethnic groups over time, violent political instability is not likely to occur in Tanzania, with its peaceful tradition and non-violent culture.

The Economy and Political Stability in Tanzania: A Summary

The first threat to political stability in the post-independence period emerged in the early 1960s from the unsatisfied demands of trade unionists. The TANU government reacted with a mixture of accommodation and suppression of the union movement. By the end of the decade, the state became increasingly authoritarian, legalising a one-party system and severely restricting civil society. In the 1970s, the introduction of various legal and institutional mechanisms helped to prevent the emergence of powerful special interest groups and the possibility of organised political opposition. The state obtained substantial control over the economy through villagisation programmes and nationalisations of major sectors.

Notwithstanding the state's increased authoritarianism, substantial improvement in its health and education services to the general population, on the one hand, and the maintenance of the party's grass-roots organisation, on the other, helped prevent the emergence of opposition and sustain political stability, especially until the 1980s. Although workers and businessmen organised strikes in the early 1970s and in the 1980s to protest against declining living standards and abuses by the parastatal managers, no major threat to political stability emerged.

The substantial economic deterioration in the 1970s arose from both exogenous shocks and policies. Compounding a series of negative exogenous shocks in the 1970s, the extension of state control over marketing and productive activities, despite weaknesses in administrative capacity, resulted in considerable inefficiency and corruption. Rural policies were not well designed and excessive state interference severely limited private incentives. As a result exports fell, foreign-aid dependency became severe, industrial capacity became grossly underused and unemployment increased. By the 1980s, the economic deterioration had undermined the state's ability to meet the basic needs of the people. Meanwhile, foreign aid declined substantially as international opinion attributed Tanzania's bad economic performance to government policies as well as its one-party regime. Thus, a wide range of institutional and economic reforms became necessary, both to permit economic recovery and to gain foreign support.

Although transition to a multiparty system did not enjoy widely based popular support, the leaders of the CCM eventually agreed that a democratic environment could help revitalise the economy, restore the links between the party and the nation and help reconstruct a socialist society. Thus, starting in 1992, the formation of political parties was permitted. Given the lack of significant social and economic segregation among the Africans, the emerging political parties could not mobilise much support, and in the first multiparty elections in 1995 the majority of the votes still favoured the CCM.

This chapter has attributed Tanzania's post-independence political stability to a large measure of socio-economic homogeneity combined with a single-party political system, with a benevolent, albeit non-democratic, leader. The achievement of political stability, however, may have partly aggravated economic problems by postponing pressures for economic reforms. Notwithstanding the inefficiencies in the system and unsustainable development policies, large amounts of foreign aid in the 1970s also helped the state to maintain political stability through the provision of basic social services.

Socio-economic inequalities will be likely to increase in the medium term as the reforms lead to an economy based on the market and the private sector. Although they probably will not threaten political stability, tensions between the Africans and the Asian minority might increase. In addition, although events since the 1980s have weakened the position of ideologists in the CCM, a sustained debate between its ideological and pragmatic factions regarding the redistributive role of the state and the size of the public sector may slow down decision making on further market reforms.

Notes

1. Tanganyika, mainland Tanzania, obtained its independence in 1961. It formed a Union with Zanzibar and was renamed Tanzania in 1964, a year after Zanzibar obtained its independence.

2. African co-operatives were permitted in 1952, with the Victoria Federation that established the alliance between the African-educated elite and the colonial state (Coulson, 1982, p. 99).

3. The Arabs constituted about 70 per cent of non-Africans, or 17 per cent of the total population, in Zanzibar in 1948 (Coulson, 1982, p. 124). They control the majority of clove production in Zanzibar, which accounts for about half of the island's GDP, and the majority of its foreign exchange earnings. Zanzibar is a major world producer of cloves.

4. On average, Zanzibar has enjoyed higher living standards and a better distribution of income than the mainland. It has suffered, however, from relying on one export commodity, cloves. The island's union with the mainland in 1964 coincided with a sharp deterioration in income from clove exports.

5. The use of the terms "pragmatists" and "ideologists" follows McHenry (1994).

6. Swahili is Arabized Bantu language and was the language of the coastal regions centuries before independence (see Hyden, 1986, p. 41 and Musti de Gennaro in Collier *et al.*, 1986, p. 122).

7. At independence, African ownership of the sisal plantations, a crop which constituted 50 per cent of exports, was 0.6 per cent, whereas Europeans held 75.3 per cent and Asians 24.1 per cent (Shivji *et al.*, 1994). Furthermore, a few thousand Europeans received ten times the agricultural credit allocated to all Africans and produced 40 per cent of the nominal agricultural output.

8. In 1959, only seven out of 299 administrative officers in the civil service were Africans (Coulson, 1982, p. 120); and, at independence, only about 25 per cent of all civil servants were African (Barkan, ed., 1984, p. 215).

9. Membership of the co-operative societies grew from 153 000 to 325 000 between 1952 and 1957 (Havnevik, 1993, p. 33).

10. By 1961, 42 per cent of the workers were unionised (Havnevik, 1993, p. 32).

11. In 1966, Africans occupied two-thirds of all senior and middle civil service posts, as compared with one quarter at independence (Hyden, 1986, p. 52).

12. After 1975, these conditions were somewhat relaxed and fringe benefits of civil servants were adjusted upwards to compensate for declining real wages.

13. *Ujamaa* stands for familyhood in Swahili. When Nyerere resigned as Prime Minister in 1962, he published a TANU pamphlet (*"Ujamaa* — The Basis of African Socialism") to describe his vision of socialism whose basis was the establishment of *ujamaa* villages for communal production and equal distribution (Havnevik, 1993, p. 196).

14. Due to the shift of emphasis in the formation of villages from establishing socialist institutions to creating economic units, *ujamaa* villages were referred to as development villages in 1974 (Migot-Adholla in Barkan, ed., 1984).

15. Hence, 37 per cent of industrial, 33 per cent of agricultural, 27 per cent of financial and 3 per cent of commercial enterprises were nationalised (McHenry, 1994, p. 131).

16. By 1981, the number of parastatals in Tanzania was about twice as great as in any other African country (McHenry, 1994, p. 130).

17. For instance, basic immunisation in Tanzania reached 75 per cent to 80 per cent (for the relevant age group) as compared with about 50 per cent in sub-Saharan Africa; infant mortality (per thousand live births) in Tanzania was 84.2 as opposed to 93.1 in sub-Saharan Africa; and the respective figures for population per hospital bed were 931 versus 1 269 (World Bank, 1995*b*).

18. Bevan *et al.* (1989) note that the decline in cash crop production since the mid-1970s is partly due to the decline in the availability of consumer goods, as well as the substitution effect resulting from the price controls that were exacerbated by an over-valued exchange rate.

19. While average real wages in the parastatal sector were 38 per cent higher than in the private sector in 1973, the trend had reversed by 1984.

20. Mwinyi was the President of Zanzibar and thus the Vice-President of Tanzania when he won 96 per cent of the votes cast.

Chapter 7

Conclusions and Policy Implications

Conclusions

This study has explored whether the contrasting experiences of violent conflict in Kenya, Uganda and Tanzania can be explained by differences in socio-economic conditions among the three countries. In the 30 years since each gained political independence, they have shown marked differences in economic and social conditions, generally to the disadvantage of Uganda.

The three countries had rather similar economic and social performances in the 1960s, the first decade after independence. The sharpest differences arose in the 1970s, when Uganda suffered considerable political and economic disruption associated with the Amin regime and reactions against it. It had strongly negative per capita economic growth, while levels of economic activity were maintained, although there was a slowdown in growth, in both Kenya and Tanzania. GDP growth per capita was slightly positive over the decade in Kenya and slightly negative in Tanzania. The political disruption in Uganda also significantly undermined government revenue, led to a rising share of expenditure on defence and reduced social expenditures sharply. By 1981, Uganda spent only 0.5 per cent of its GDP on health and education in the public sector, compared with 8.1 per cent in Kenya. Tanzanian revenue collection lagged behind that of Kenya, but Tanzania still considerably outperformed Uganda on social expenditure.

These large differences in macroeconomic performance and in social expenditures moderated in the 1980s and reversed in the 1990s. Uganda again had major political disruptions in the mid-1980s, but after that as political stability returned economic growth resumed. Tanzania had a bad decade economically in the 1980s, confronting severe foreign exchange shortages due to poor export performance, rising debt and disrupted external assistance as the donor community tried to persuade the government to change its highly interventionist economic policies towards more market-oriented ones. In the 1990s, Uganda outperformed the other two countries, despite marked improvements in Tanzanian performance, while Kenya mostly had very poor performance with falling per capita incomes. Nonetheless, Kenya maintained a high share of national income going to the social sectors, while spending proportionately less on defence than Uganda (still subject to ongoing conflict in the North) and Tanzania.

Differences in social development broadly reflected those in economic performance and government expenditure over these years. Uganda lagged badly up to 1980 on all indicators compared with Kenya and on most compared with Tanzania. Kenya made quite impressive progress towards universal coverage of health and education services while Tanzania did so for primary education and basic health services. Again some reversal in these differences occurred from the mid-1980s. By 1990, calorie availability was better in Uganda than Kenya, with secondary school enrolment and doctor availability better than Tanzania's; but it still lagged severely on infant mortality rates, adult literacy and access to safe water.

Kenya and Uganda experienced considerable differences in economic and social conditions across regions. Over the years both saw some narrowing of regional differentials. In Uganda, however, this narrowing remained confined to services while inequality of employment and incomes grew. In both countries, the centre had relative privilege in access to services, employment and incomes, with the North relatively deprived. In Kenya this deprivation was confined to a small proportion of the population (only 2 per cent, in the most consistently deprived province, the Northeast). Nyanza (17 per cent of the population), also relatively disadvantaged, did enjoy rising incomes along with the rest of the country. In Uganda the general regression made the impact of inequalities worse and the most destitute region, the North, accounted for 20 per cent of the population (1969). Uganda has a significantly higher population per hectare than Kenya, but landlessness is greater and a more central political issue in Kenya.

Kenya developed a much more integrated economy, by any measure, and a more vibrant private sector both in agriculture and elsewhere. These features, plus much more extensive secondary and higher education, led to the emergence of a larger middle class, which on the whole managed to prosper for much of the period. Disaffected classes did not gain, however, including those suffering rising rural poverty who are landless or have very small farms, and the urban poor encompassing the urban informal sector and unemployed youth.

Tanzania's policies under Nyerere aimed deliberately and explicitly towards inclusive and egalitarian patterns of development. Income distribution was more equal than in the other two countries. Regional inequalities in public services appear much smaller than in Kenya but above Uganda's in primary education (Table 7.1).

Table 7.1. **Measures of Inequality in Kenya, Uganda and Tanzania**

Measure	Uganda	Kenya	Tanzania
Per cent of income received by the bottom 40 per cent			
early 1970s	N/A	8.9 (1974)	16 (1969)
early 1990s	17.1	10.1	17.8
Gini coefficient, early 1990s	40.8	57.5	38.1
Coefficient of variation in primary education services across areas:		0.455 (1968)	0.087 (1968)
	0.231 (1993)	0.417 (1980)	0.109 (1990)

Sources: World Bank, *World Development Reports*; previous tables in this study.

The many economic and social disadvantages suffered by Uganda might appear to explain its violence, but the situation is not so straightforward. Poor macroeconomic performance *followed* rather than preceded the most horrendous episodes of violence. Amin and then Obote II largely bore responsibility for instigating violence, which in turn led to economic regression. Political issues — power seeking, deep fault lines left by the colonial era especially concerning the role of Buganda, and subsequent retaliatory violence — had the greatest relevance, but these were salient precisely because of inequalities and economic policy failures. The economic privileges of the Centre pitted it politically and in the national mentality against the rest of the country. Economic failures provided conditions ripe for the continuation of violence because people had so little to lose from a breakdown in the economic system, such as it was. The same factors influence the chronic violence that besets the North today. Uganda also suffered from destabilising external influences which supported its opposition forces, while both Kenya and Tanzania received external help which mainly bolstered the established order against rebellious political violence.

The major episodes of violence in Kenya also stemmed from economic factors. The *Mau Mau* rebellion erupted in direct response to the way settlers took Kikuyu land and left Kikuyu as squatters in intolerable conditions. The Shifta wars of the 1960s took place in the deprived Northeast which gained almost nothing from its adherence to the Kenyan state. The high and rising crime rate today represents a form of economic protest against rising inequality and poverty. Despite these incidents, however, Kenya has enjoyed general stability with little violence in comparison to Uganda's. This too almost certainly has an economic and social explanation. The development process incorporated most people as the economy prospered and social services were extended. The developing private sector, with a growing community of middle-sized farmers resulting from land entitlement programmes and parallel developments in industry and services, extended vested interests in stability to a sizeable middle class. While the Moi regime has practically disenfranchised the Kikuyu politically, they retain many of their economic privileges.

Tanzania, considerably poorer than Kenya, had a much worse economic record in aggregate terms up to 1980. Its failed economic policies left it with a relatively small middle class and, like Uganda, a large subsistence sector. From a purely macroeconomic perspective, one would have expected to see Tanzania more prone to violence than Kenya. Moreover, Tanzania has had relatively low economic integration, more than Uganda during the 1970s but less than Kenya. For example, the middle classes in the 1980s accounted for about 9 per cent of the population, half the estimated proportion of Uganda and only about a third of that of Kenya[1].

Yet of the three countries, Tanzania has been the most stable, avoiding even the relatively minor outbreaks suffered by Kenya. Its inclusive and egalitarian policies can partly claim responsibility, along with some historical and political factors. The colonial inheritance left a less segregated society with few sharp economic divisions among tribes and a national language, features which neither of the other two countries shared. Moreover, the smaller size of the largest tribes meant less intense rivalry between particular tribes. The wise political leadership of Nyerere, aiming above all at inclusiveness and national unity, in complete contrast to the explicitly divisive policies followed by Obote and — to a much lesser extent — by Kenyatta and Moi, also contributed significantly. Yet while differences in political leadership arose partly from the characters of the respective leaders, they also responded to political systems and their economic and ethnic contexts. In Uganda, party politics have tended to dissolve into ethnic politics as the most effective way of securing power. This has happened in Kenya too whenever elections take place with more than one political party. Tanzania had a single party for most of the period, with multiparty politics starting only in 1992, subsequently showing some tendency for political parties to develop along regional and ethnic lines.

This study contends that economic-inspired violence requires both leaders and followers to perceive that there is so little to lose from it that the potential gains outweigh the losses. In Uganda this often held true because economic opportunities outside the state were so slight that control over the state became all-important; peasants received so little from the state in social or economic benefits that they could retreat into subsistence with relatively little loss. In Kenya, on the other hand, potential leaders could prosper even without political power, while large numbers of peasants gained enough from the system to make stability desirable. Stratification was vertical, with the very poor and the middle class to be found in a number of ethnic groups. Hence the coincidence of ethnicity with economic motivation for political violence remained much less marked than in Uganda. Tanzania incorporated members of different ethnic groups into its large civil service and made comprehensive the benefits from its expanding basic services. While the gains lessened and even reversed over the late 1970s and early 1980s, groups shared emergent losses evenly. The gains from violence appeared small.

Policy Recommendations

The key economic condition for stability — equitable growth — is straightforward if difficult to obtain, especially in conditions of instability. Growth must encompass people from different regions and ethnicities and benefit them economically and socially, i.e. it must promote *horizontal* equality; it needs to provide sufficient public services for the state to be worth supporting, while engendering a dynamic private sector which provides a route to prosperity not mainly dependent on the state. Policies must:

— expand social and economic infrastructure with regional balance and special efforts in deprived regions;

— provide the conditions for a dynamic, legal private sector, removing regulations and distortions that lead to illegal parallel markets, reforming property rights, and promoting institutional reform to extend credit widely;

— support ethnic and regional balance in the government, public sector employment including the army, and, where necessary, the private sector (as with the "Kenyanisation" efforts or the New Economic Policy in Malaysia); and

— avoid cutbacks in social and economic expenditures, especially in vulnerable regions, which may demand higher taxation and less spending on defence, administration and prestige projects.

In addition, countries with potential or actual ethnic problems need to make a huge effort to educate people to live and work together. Civic education should form a large element in all educational activities, including schools, radio, TV, newspapers, churches and so on, while education in the opposite direction should be outlawed. Tanzania has outlawed tribal, religious and racial discrimination in its constitution.

Policy recommendations for outsiders — neighbours, aid donors, NGOs, etc. — include:

— not supporting destabilising activities with finance or arms;

— enforcing aid and economic and social conditionality which supports the policies described above, especially emphasising *inclusive* economic and social policies and avoiding cutbacks in expenditure on social and economic infrastructure. In practice, this might conflict with normal structural adjustment policies, for example avoiding cutbacks on infrastructure expenditure, or pursuing regional balance in employment and expenditure policies which could conflict with "efficiency" considerations;

— crafting any political conditionality with sensitivity to the potential for conflict, and supporting democracy in politically vulnerable societies only in ways which include strong protection for minority rights and the outlawing of discrimination. Democratic forms alone will not resolve and may even cause political violence.

As political vulnerability extends to more and more countries, governments and external agencies need to give conscious priority to policies that will lessen the likelihood of conflict. It does not suffice to assume that policies promoting economic efficiency and political democracy will automatically achieve this.

Note

1. Estimates of Berg-Schlosser and Siegler (1990). The "middle classes" include large-scale farmers, the *petite bourgeoisie*, the state class, managers, capitalists and the salariat in these data.

Bibliography

Africa Confidential (various issues).

AFRICA WATCH (1993), *State Sponsored Ethnic Conflict in Kenya,* Washington, D.C.

AMNESTY INTERNATIONAL (1985), *Uganda Six Years After Amin,* Amnesty International, London.

AMNESTY INTERNATIONAL (1992), *Uganda: The Failure to Safeguard Human Rights*, Amnesty International, London.

AVIRGAN, T. and M. HONEY (1982), *War in Uganda*, Tanzania Publishing House, Dar es Salaam.

BANK OF TANZANIA (1983), *Tanzania: Twenty Years of Independence (1961-1981),* Government Printer, Dar-es-Salaam.

BARKAN, J.D. (ed.) (1984), *Politics and Public Policy in Kenya and Tanzania*, Heinemann, Nairobi.

BARROW, E. (1995), "Education in Turkana", *The Pastoralist*, No. 6, September.

BERG-SCHLOSSER, D. and R. SIEGLER (1990), *Political Stability and Development: A Comparative Analysis of Kenya, Tanzania and Uganda*, Lynne Rienner, Boulder and London.

BEVAN, D., P. COLLIER and P. HORSNELL (1989), "The Case of Tanzania", *in The Supply of Manufactured Goods and Agricultural Development*, OECD Development Centre Papers, OECD, Paris.

BIENEN, H. (1974), *Kenya: The Politics of Participation and Control,* Princeton University Press, Princeton, NJ.

BIGSTEN, A. (1977), "Regional Inequality in Kenya", IDS, University of Nairobi Working Paper No. 330, Nairobi.

BIGSTEN, A. (1995), "Uganda 1995: Boom and Poverty in Uganda", *Macro-economic Studies,* SIDA, Stockholm.

BRETT, E.A. (1993), *Providing for the Rural Poor: Institutional Decay and Transformation in Uganda*, Fountain Publishers, Kampala.

BWENGYE, F.L. (1985), *The Agony of Uganda: From Idi Amin to Obote: Repressive Rule and Bloodshed*, Regency Press, London.

CHAZAN, N., R. MORTIMER, J. RAVENHILL and D. ROTHSCHILD (1992), *Politics and Society in Contemporary Africa*, Lynne Rienner, Boulder.

CHAZAN, N. and D. ROTHSCHILD (1988), *The Precarious Balance: State and Society*, Westview Press, Boulder.

COHEN, A, (1959), *British Policy in Changing Africa*, Routledge and Kegan Paul, London.

COLLIER, P. *et al.* (1986), *Labor and Poverty in Rural Tanzania*, Clarendon Press, Oxford.

COULSON, A. (1982), *Tanzania: A Political Economy*, Clarendon Press, Oxford.

DODGE, C.P. and P.D. WEIBE (eds) (1985), *Uganda: The Breakdown of Health Services*, Pergamon Press, Oxford.

FENDRU, I. (1985), "The Rural Question and Democracy in Uganda", *Mazuro* 6, No. 1.

Financial Times, 20 August 1997.

FUREDI, F. (1992), *The Mau Mau War in Perspective*, James Currey, London.

FURLEY, O. (1989), "Britain and Uganda: From Amin to Museveni", *in* K. RUPESINGHE (ed.), *Conflict Resolution in Uganda*, James Currey, London.

GALLI, R.E. (ed.) (1981), *The Political Economy of Rural Development, Peasants, International Capital and the State*, State University of New York Press, New York.

GERTZEL, C. (1970), *The Politics of Independent Kenya 1963-1968,* Northwestern University Press, Evanston.

GIBBON, P. (1995), *Markets, Civil Society and Democracy in Kenya,* Scandinavian Institute of African Studies, Uppsala.

GREEN, R. (1981), "Magendo in the Political Economy of Uganda: Pathology, Parallel System or Dominant Sub-mode of Production", *IDS Discussion Paper No. 164*, Institute of Development Studies, Sussex.

HANSEN, H.B. and M. TWADDLE (eds) (1988), *Uganda Now: Between Decay and Development*, James Currey, London.

HAVNEVIK, K.J. *et al.* (1988), *Tanzania: Country Study and Norwegian Aid Review*, University of Bergen, Bergen.

HAVNEVIK, K.J. (1993), *Tanzania: The Limits to Development from Above*, Nordiska Afrikainstitutet and Mkuki na Nyota Publishers, Uppsala.

HEYER, J. (1990), *Kenya: Monitoring Living Conditions and Consumption Patterns,* UNRISD, Geneva.

HOLMQUIST, F., F. WEAVER and M. FORD (1994), "The Structural Development of Kenya's Political Economy", *African Studies Review,* Volume 37, No. 1 (April).

HUMPHREYS, F. (1996), *"A Cross-country Statistical Analysis of the Effects of War on Developing Countries"*, Extended Essay for the M. Sc. in Economics for Development, University of Oxford, Oxford.

HUNT, D. (1996), "The Social and Economic Impacts of Individual Land Titling", *in* MBEERE, *Eastern Kenya*, IDS, University of Nairobi Working Paper No. 505, Nairobi.

HYDEN, G. (1986), "TANU Yagenja Nchi: Political Development in Rural Tanzania", *Lund Political Studies 8*, Scandinavian University Books, Lund.

IKIARA, G., M. JAMA and J. AMADI (1995), "The Cereals Chain in Kenya: Actors, Reforms and Politics", *in* P. GIBBON (ed.) (1995), *Markets, Civil Society and Democracy in Kenya*, Scandinavian Institute of African Studies, Uppsala.

ILO (1982), *Basic Needs in Danger, A Basic Needs Oriented Strategy for Tanzania*, ILO/ JASPA, Addis Ababa.

JAMAL, V. (1991), "Inequalities and Adjustment in Uganda", *Development and Change*, 22.

KANYINGA, K. (1996), "Struggles of Access to Land", IDS, University of Nairobi Working Paper No. 504.

KAPLINSKY, R. (1978), "Trends in the Distribution of Income in Kenya, 1966-1976", IDS, University of Nairobi Working Paper No. 336.

KARUGIRE, S. (1980), *A Political History of Uganda*, Heinemann Educational Books, Nairobi.

KASFIR, N. (1988), "Land and Peasants in Western Uganda Bushenyi and Mbarara Districts", *in* H. HANSEN and M. TWADDLE (eds), *Uganda Now: Between Decay and Development*, James Currey, London.

KENYA HUMAN RIGHTS COMMISSION (1995), *Quarterly Repression Report*, Nairobi.

KENYA NATIONAL Council for POPULATION AND DEVELOPMENT, CENTRAL BUREAU OF STATISTICS AND MACRO INTERNATIONAL (1993), *Kenya Demographic and Health Survey*, Nairobi.

KHIDDU-MAKABUYA, E. (1989), "Paramilitarism and Human Rights", *in* K. RUPESINGHE (ed.), *Conflict Resolution in Uganda*, James Currey, London.

KHIDDU-MAKABUYA, E. (1991), "The Rule of Law and Human Rights in Uganda: The Missing Link", *in* H.B. HANSEN and M. TWADDLE (eds), *Changing Uganda*, James Currey, London.

KIGULA, J. (1993), "Land Disputes in Uganda: An Overview of the Types of Land Disputes and the Dispute Settlement Fora", mimeo, Makerere Institute of Social Research, Kampala.

KIGULA, J. (1996), *Land Disputes in Uganda (Volume I): District Surveys*, mimeo, Makerere Institute of Social Research/Land Tenure Centre, Kampala.

KLUGMAN, J. (1996), *Socio-economic Sources of Conflict in Kenya*, paper prepared for OECD Development Centre, Paris.

LELE, U. and R. MEYERS (1989), *Growth and Structural Change in East Africa*, Madia Discussion Paper 3, The World Bank, Washington, D.C.

MAALIM, D. (1995), "Insecurity and Underdevelopment in Northeastern Kenya", *in* A. UMAR (ed.), *Sustainable Development for North East Kenya*, Crescent of Hope, Nairobi.

MAMDANI, M. (1976), *Politics and Class Formation in Uganda*, Monthly Review Press, London.

MAMDANI, M. (1988), "NRA/NRM; Two Years in Power", Text of a Public Lecture at Makerere University, 3 March 1988, Kampala, Progressive Publishing House.

Mamdani, M. (1996), *Citizen and Subject: Contemporary Africa and the Legacy of Late Colonialism*, Princeton University Press, Princeton, NJ.

McHenry, D.E. (1994), *Limited Choices: The Political Struggle for Socialism in Tanzania*, Lynne Rienner Publishers, Boulder, Colorado.

Middleton, V. and A. Rassam (eds) (1990), *Encyclopaedia of World Culture*, Vol. IX, *Africa and the Middle East*, G.K. Hall and Co, Boston.

Moshi, H. (1992), *Zum Entwicklungsbeitrag Staatlicher in den Entwicklungländern: Dargestellt am Beispiel Tanzania*, Nomos, Baden Baden.

Mudoola, D. (1988), "Political Transitions Since Amin: A Study in Political Pathology", *in* H.B. Hansen and M. Twaddle (eds), *Uganda Now: Between Decay and Development*, James Currey, London.

Mudoola, D. (1992), "Interest Groups and Institution Building Processes in Uganda, 1962-71", Makerere Institute of Social Research, Kampala.

Mugai, G. (1995), "Ethnicity and the Renewal of Competitive Politics in Kenya", Chapter 5 *in* H. Glickman (ed.), *Ethnic Conflict and Democratisation in Africa*, The African Studies Association Press, Atlanta, Georgia.

Mullins, J.D. (1904), *The Wonderful Story of Uganda*, Church Missionary Society, London.

Mutibwa, P. (1992), *Uganda Since Independence; A Story of Unfulfilled Hopes*, Fountain Publishers, Kampala.

Nelson, H. (ed.) (1986), *Kenya: A Country Study*, The American University, Washington, D.C.

Njuguna, M. (1995), "Development Finance in Kenya's Industrial Sector: A Political Economy Approach", Institute of Development Studies, University of Nairobi, Working Paper 499.

Nowrojee, B. (1993), "Divide and Rule: State Sponsored Ethnic Violence in Kenya", Human Rights Watch, New York, NY.

Nsibanbi, A.R. (1989), *"The Land Question and Conflict" in* K. Rupesinghe (ed).

Okoth, P. (1996), "The Historical Dimensions of Democracy in Uganda: A Review of the Problems and Prospects", *in* J. Oloka-Onyango *et al.*, *Law and the Struggle for Democracy in East Africa*, Claripress, Nairobi.

Oloka-Onyango, J. (1990), "Police Powers, Human Rights and the State in Kenya and Uganda: A Comparative Analysis", *Third World Legal Studies*.

Republic of Kenya (1981, 1984, 1985) *Statistical Abstracts*, Central Bureau of Statistics, Nairobi.

Republic of Kenya (1992), *Population Census 1989*, Central Bureau of Statistics, Nairobi.

Republic of Kenya (1994), *Report of the Public Accounts Committee for the Year 1993/94*, Vol. 1, Central Bureau of Statistics, Nairobi.

Republic of Kenya (1996), *Welfare Monitoring Survey II 1994 Basic Report*, Central Bureau of Statistics, Nairobi.

REPUBLIC OF UGANDA (1966), *National Consultative Council Debates*, Vol. 4, Government Printer, Entebbe.

REPUBLIC OF UGANDA (1966*a*), *Statistical Abstract 1996*, Government Printer, Entebbe.

REPUBLIC OF UGANDA (1966*b*), *Work for Progress: Uganda's Second Five Year Plan*, Government Printer, Entebbe.

REPUBLIC OF UGANDA (1971*a*), *Statistical Abstract 1971*, Department of Statistics, MFEP, Kampala.

REPUBLIC OF UGANDA (1971*b*), *The Birth of the Second Republic*, Government Printer, Entebbe.

REPUBLIC OF UGANDA (1972), *Uganda's Third Five Year Development Plan 1971/2-1975/6*, Government Printer, Entebbe.

REPUBLIC OF UGANDA (1973), *Report on the 1969 Population Census*, Vol. III, Government Printer, Entebbe.

REPUBLIC OF UGANDA (1991), *Uganda Population and Housing Census*, Government Printer, Entebbe.

REPUBLIC OF UGANDA (1996*a*), Ministry of Finance and Economic Planning (MFEP), *Report on the Uganda National Integrated Household Survey, 1992-3*, Vol. III, MFEP, Kampala.

REPUBLIC OF UGANDA (1996*b*), *Statistical Abstract 1996*, Government Printer, Entebbe.

REPUBLIC OF UGANDA (1996*c*), Cabinet Committee Reporting on "Land Disputes in Kasese District", Kampala.

RUPESINGHE, K. (ed.) (1989), *Conflict and Resolution in Uganda*, International Peace Research Institute, Oslo.

SHIPTON, P. (1988), "The Kenyan Land Tenure Reform: Misunderstandings in the Public Creation of Private Property", *in* R.E. DOWNS and S.P. REYNA (eds), *Land and Society in Contemporary Africa*, University Press of New England, Hanover.

SHIVJI, I.G. with Sweden Direktorat for Utviklingshjelp and Norway Direktorat for Utviklingshjelp (1994), "A Legal Quagmire: Tanzania's Regulation of Land Tenure (Establishment of Villages) (Act 1992)", International Institute for Environment and Development, London.

SIVARD, R. (1993), *World Military and Social Expenditures 1993*, World Priorities, Washington, D.C.

SORA, H. (1995), "Northern Kenya: A Historical Perspective", *in* A. UMAR (ed.), *Sustainable Development for North East Kenya*, Crescent of Hope, Nairobi.

STEWART, F. (1986), *Economic Policies and Agricultural Performance: The Case of Tanzania*, OECD Development Centre Papers, OECD Development Centre, Paris.

STEWART, F. (1997), *The Economic Factors Contributing to Conflict in Uganda, 1961-1996*, paper prepared for the OECD Development Centre, Paris.

The Observer, 5 January 1997.

The Standard, 19 June 1992.

THROUP, D. (1996), *The Triumph of the System: The Kenyan Struggle for Multiparty Democracy*, James Currey, London.

Uganda Herald, 24 April 1952.

UMAR, A. (ed.) (1995), *Sustainable Development for North East Kenya*, Crescent of Hope, Nairobi.

UNDP, *Human Development Report*, various editions.

UNDP (1996), *Uganda's Human Development Report*, UNDP, Kampala.

UNICEF/ODA/AMREF (1995), *Participatory Poverty Assessment Study*, June, Nairobi.

VON FREYHOLD, M. (1979), *Ujamaa Villages in Tanzania*, Monthly Review Press, New York.

WALLIS, C. (1953), *Report of an Inquiry into African Local Government in the Protectorate of Uganda*, Government Printer, Entebbe.

WEEKS, W. and C. YOUNG (1996), *Conflict Management in Kenya*, report prepared for USAID, Nairobi, Kenya.

WORLD BANK (1975), "Bureaucrats in Business: The Economics and Politics of Government Ownership", World Bank Policy Research Report, O.U.P. New York, NY.

WORLD BANK (1983a), *Kenya Growth and Structural Change*, World Bank Country Study, Washington, D.C.

WORLD BANK (1983b), *Kenya Land Issues Paper*, Report No. 4391-KE, Washington, D.C.

WORLD BANK (1988), *Employment and Growth in Kenya*, Report No. 7293-KE, Washington, D.C.

WORLD BANK (1989), *African Economic and Financial Data*, Washington, D.C.

WORLD BANK (1990a), *The Long-term Perspective Study of Sub-Saharan Africa*, Background Papers, Washington, D.C.

WORLD BANK (1990b), *World Bank/Tanzania Relations, 1961-1987*, Report No. 8329, Washington, D.C.

WORLD BANK (1992a), *Kenya Private Sector Assessment*, Vols. 1 and 2, Washington, D.C.

WORLD BANK (1992b), *Kenya Local Government Finance Study*, Report No. 8997-KE, Washington, D.C.

WORLD BANK (1993a), *Uganda: Social Sectors*, Washington, D.C.

WORLD BANK (1993b), *Kenya Employment Growth for Poverty Alleviation*, Washington, D.C.

WORLD BANK (1995a), *Kenya Poverty Assessment*, Report No. 13152-KE, Washington, D.C.

WORLD BANK (1995b), *Social Indicators*, Washington, D.C.

WORLD BANK, (1996a), *African Development Indicators 1996*, World Bank, Washington, D.C.

WORLD BANK, (1996b), *Uganda: The Challenge of Growth and Poverty Reduction*, Washington, D.C.

WORLD BANK (1996c), *The Challenge of Reforms: Growth, Incomes and Welfare*, Report No. 14982, Washington, D.C.

WORLD BANK (1997), *World Development Indicators*, Washington, D.C.

WORLD BANK (various), *World Development Report*, various editions, Washington, D.C.

OECD PUBLICATIONS, 2, rue André-Pascal, 75775 PARIS CEDEX 16
PRINTED IN FRANCE
(41 1999 10 1 P) ISBN 92-64-17141-X – No. 50953 1999